EDUCATOR'S WORLD WIDE WEB TOURGUIDE

A GRAPHICAL TOUR OF OVER 200 EDUCATIONAL TREASURES ON THE WORLD WIDE WEB

■   ■   ■

By the staff of *Classroom Connect,* the premier
Internet newsletter for K-12 educators

Gregory Giagnocavo, Editorial Director
Tim McLain, Writer
Vince DiStefano, Writer
Chris Noonan Sturm, Editor
Eileen Mauskapf, Assistant Editor and Indexer

Wentworth Worldwide Media, Inc.
1866 Colonial Village Lane, Lancaster, PA 17601
(717) 393-1000
Email: connect@wentworth.com
URL: http://www.wentworth.com

Dedicated to the schools, educators, and students who are contributing to and using the World Wide Web to take education to new heights.

From the publishers of

Library of Congress Catalog Card Number: ISBN: 0-932577-16-4
Printed in the United States of America

For information about bulk sales and *Classroom Connect* products and seminars, call 800-638-1639.
Email to: connect@wentworth.com   URL: http://www.wentworth.com

All terms mentioned in this book that are known to be trademarks or service marks have been appropriately capitalized.

Cover design and illustration: Daniel Delis Hill
Designers: Angie Neifert, Carol Sweigart, Amy L. Wiggins, and Natalie A. Zuch
Proofing: Sheryl Mills
Media relations: Kim Conlin

Library of Congress Cataloging in Publication Data

Educator's World Wide Web tourguide : Classroom connect's guide to the
    best 150 web sites for K-12 education / by the staff of Classroom
    connect ; Gregory Giagnocavo, editorial director; Tim McLain,
    writer; Vince DiStefano, writer; Chris Noonan Sturm, editor.
            p. cm.
        Includes index.
        ISBN 0-932577-16-4 (pbk.)
            1. Education—Computer network resources—Directories.
    2. World Wide Web (Information retrieval system)—Directories.
    I. Giagnocavo, Gregory, 1953- . II. McLain, Tim, 1970- .
    III. DiStefano, Vince, 1970- . IV. Sturm, Chris Noonan.
    V. Series: Classroom connect.
    LB1044.87.E38   1995
    025.06'37—dc20   95-24237
                                                CIP

CONTENTS

HOW THE WEB BRINGS A "LIVING TEXTBOOK" TO SCHOOLS

The Internet's growing educational potential

The Internet has been called many things—including difficult to use. But many thousands of educators have overcome that challenge and been richly rewarded by a wealth of educational resources. Now, thanks to the proliferation in the past year of graphical World Wide Web software, educators and students can enjoy an ease of use and a level of excitement that's never before been a part of the Internet.

Recently, educators the world over have begun to realize that the World Wide Web is more than just an easier way to navigate the Internet. They've discovered that the Web actually adds personality, depth, and breadth to the information on the Internet. And the ease with which new information can be added, often with graphics, sound, and video (and real-time audio and video by 1996), has unleashed legions of a new breed of electronic publishers who energetically mount reams of new information on the Web every day. This new type of publisher includes international experts, historians, business professionals, teachers, research lab scientists, universities, libraries, medical centers...and thousands of K-12 students!

The Living Textbook Concept

In presentations to educators across North America, I've shared my vision of the enormous potential of tightly integrating the use of the Internet into the classroom curriculum. A "classroom without books" may not be a reality for decades, yet each school day educators wrestle with textbooks that are often out of date as soon as they're delivered, texts that are by their very nature limited in the amount of information they can present. Consider the many updates textbooks would require to reflect the recent changes in international politics and geographic boundaries, as well as advances in medicine, science, and technology. It hasn't been possible for traditional publishers to accommodate these up-to-the minute, rapid-fire developments. And since textbooks aren't replaced every year, it's all too common for teachers to become frustrated with the amount of old, inaccurate, and limited information in classroom textbooks, curriculum materials, and teacher manuals.

But imagine this...suppose every textbook contained pointers to Internet resources that focused on a particular subject. Do you want students to access the latest information about a particular subject or topic, no matter what has just occurred in that field of study? Simply jump to the corresponding Web page and read about, discover, study, and explore an almost unlimited number of topic-specific and related resources. Better yet, students can download, save, print out, or build their own multimedia presentations of the information they discover.

Imagine the possibilities. Recently discovered but long-hidden documents, pictures, and artifacts bring history to life; message postings from world-class research scientists add a human element to the latest scientific discovery; sound, video, and graphics make the study of geography and world cultures come alive. Immediate coverage of world events, sports, politics, and on-the-spot reports from the scene of natural disasters give new meaning to a class on current events. It could be years until traditional printed materials reflect this information. But for users on the World Wide Web, it's all just a mouse click away.

That's what I refer to as the "living textbook" concept—textbooks and classroom materials that are never really out of date because they are linked to the Internet. Each chapter or study unit will have topic-specific pointers to a variety of Internet resources including newsgroups, mailing lists, and Web addresses.

Student homework and class projects will begin to incorporate rich resources available online, driven in large part by these text references to the related information available online. And the rich resources of the Web will play a most important role in the implementation of this concept. For educators and students—and parents—the Net's constantly updated ebb and flow of information assures that the "latest and greatest" is always online.

How soon will traditional textbook and curriculum publishers recognize this and begin the transition to "living textbooks"? It may take a few more years. The Internet is rapidly becoming the distribution medium of choice, the essential backbone of the Information Superhighway. But the fluid nature of the Internet also means having to deal with ever-changing site addresses, and finding topic-specific educational sites takes time—both are challenges for most educators.

The Internet itself is considered to be almost 20 years old. But for K-12 educators, it's only in its infancy. We've only had a brief glimpse of the excitement that the World Wide Web will deliver in the next two years. Get ready for an incredible journey.

Gregory Giagnocavo
Email to: jgg@wentworth.com

P.S. You don't have to wait for publishers to create "living textbooks." You can adopt the concept right now, with a minimum of effort. This book is a resource to help you locate appropriate Internet resources that you can use and recommend with confidence. It's organized into curriculum subject areas, with curriculum integration ideas and pointers to related online resources. This book will help you bring timely resources, and excitement, into the classroom.

That's why we wanted to publish a Web book for educators—it's your key to tapping the incredible educational potential of the Internet, in particular, the World Wide Web. A quick glance through these pages will help you see how easily you can begin integrating the Internet into your educational activities.

THE WEB OF REAL LIFE

Shelve those CD-ROMs, because now you can turn your school's computer on to the biggest, most vibrant CD-ROM of all—the Internet's World Wide Web.

The Web is real life, not pre-packaged information. It's multimedia information in the raw—text, graphics, video, and sound—that challenges students to think critically and analytically to turn it into knowledge. That's education for life.

Students can find virtually anything on the Web. Government documents, biographies of scientists or authors, data on space shuttle missions, dictionaries of Shakespearean English, news magazine articles, song lyrics from every musical era, classical art. More is added every day. For the past two or three years, Web usage and sites are estimated to have grown by 300 to 400 percent, and it's still growing.

Schools all over the world are part of that growth. More than 450 K-12 schools in the United States have home pages that a user of one of the 30 million computers connected to the Internet may read. Schools in Canada, Australia, Sweden, and other countries are also reaching out to each other and the rest of the world via the Web.

What are schools putting on their Web pages? School news, faculty biographies, student newspapers, student home pages, favorite Web sites, reports on class projects, news for young people, descriptions of their communities, stories about how they put up their pages; the list could go on.

School statistics on the Web

Web66's Registry of K-12 Schools on the Web features a clickable U.S. map and a hyperlinked list of countries so you can easily visit schools all over the world.
> **URL: http://web66.coled.umn.edu/schools.html**

Want to find out how many schools are on the Web and in which states? Check out John and Janice's Research Page. The school Web site addresses are hyperlinked so all you need do is click on them to visit.
> **URL: http://k12.cnidr.org/janice_k12/states/states.html**

Gleason Sackman, a K-12 educator and Internet pioneer, keeps a running list of all K-12 schools, districts, and state boards of education on the Internet.
> **URL: http://www.ndsu.nodak.edu/k12**

The Web world

The Web is active, not passive. Students don't simply retrieve information from it, they create it. The exciting thing about the Web right now is that there is no standard for content. This is an evolving medium of delivering information, and schools, educators, and students can be part of that evolution. When a boy, girl, or teacher in Iowa or Australia comes up with a new idea for their school's Web page, they can instantly post it so everyone who uses the Internet can judge it on its own merits.

The content and design of Web pages and sites run the gamut. Some Web sites, such as the U.S. government's FedWorld, are vast repositories of data or information. Others, such as Myths and Legends, are unique, intellectually stimulating experiences that showcase the multimedia capabilities of the medium. Some focus on a very specific subject or purpose, such as Carlos' Online Coloring Book.

Whatever their focus, Web sites will surprise you with unexpected information that leaps out of corners, so set your expectations aside. That's part of the fascination of the Web. Unlike a book, which you can skim to find out what's ahead, you never know what's behind the next click of the mouse at a Web site. It demands exploration. Some educators are concerned that when students explore the Web they gloss over information, preferring to hyperlink their way from site to site without really *learning* anything. That's the challenge the Web holds for educators—they must teach students to delve deeply, think critically, and analyze constantly as they use the Web to find and sift through information to fulfill an educational task.

The entire World Wide Web demands exploration, and that takes time. The purpose of this book is to point educators and students to Web sites that are valuable for a range of subjects. Visit them, add them to your bookmarks, perhaps even make some of them part of your school's Web page.

When your school is ready to put its home page on the World Wide Web, you can turn to *Classroom Connect*. Schools that don't have the technology to put their pages on the Internet can mount them free on our World Wide Web site in an area called ClassroomWeb. Any school can submit up to two 8 1/2 x 11-inch Web pages, formatted in HTML, with up to two GIF images per page (50k or less each). Send your pages and graphics on disk by mail to *Classroom Connect*, P.O. Box 10488, Lancaster PA 17605-0488. Or attach them to an email message.

> **Email to: classweb@wentworth.com**
> Type **School Web Page** in the subject line, and put your school's name, teacher's name, address, phone number, and email address in the message.

To see what more than 150 schools have done with their Web pages, visit ClassroomWeb at the following address.
> **URL: http://www.wentworth.com/classweb**

> Chris Noonan Sturm
> Editor
> **Email to: cnsturm@wentworth.com**

HOW THE BOOK AND CD-ROM ARE ORGANIZED

The *Educator's World Wide Web TourGuide* is designed to give K-12 educators immense value in quick bites. We've written and designed it so you can easily find what you want. We've crammed each page with information you can use in the classroom. This is more than just a book full of Web sites. Here's why.

The chapters

The book is divided into 11 chapters by subject matter so you know where to find the educational Web sites you need. The sites in each chapter are listed at the beginning of the chapter. Each chapter includes at least one general resource, which you'll find marked with this icon: 📖 . This general resource site is an index or database you can use to search the Web for information on a specific subject.

So you can experience the Web in its color glory, we've included a glossy, 16-page section of full-color computer screen shots of 48 Web sites. While the sites have educational value, we also chose them for their graphic value. Several of the sites also appear elsewhere in the book.

The pages

Each page in this book is a self-contained package of information about one Web site. Our writers/Internet navigators took care to select sites that have great value for educators. New sites come online every day, and not all of them are worth your time. We've included only the best.

On each page you'll find the name of the site, its URL address, a look at a page from the site, and a description of the site's value to educators. To help you apply the site in the classroom, each page includes one or two ideas for how you might use the site with your students. Lastly, each page also includes a list of three or four other sites that have related information. For example, if the site featured on the page is about volcanoes, we've listed other places on the Internet where you can find information about volcanoes.

Counting all the sites on each page and in the color section, you'll find more than 500 educational Internet sites referenced in this book!

The appendix, glossary, and index

The appendix, *Questions and Answers about the World Wide Web,* is a primer about the Web. Its Q & A format allows you to scan it quickly for the questions you need answered. More accomplished Web navigators will find pointers to information about Web software. The Glossary provides definitions of Internet and World Wide Web terms.

The book also includes a list of sites and a subject index. The Site List is an alphabetical list of every site referenced in the book and is divided by chapter. The sites in the Color Section are included. The Index is a subject index to the matter covered in the book.

The CD-ROM

The *TourGuide* includes a CD-ROM readable by Macintosh and Windows computers and packed with education Web sites and other helpful information. Consult the *ReadMe.txt* file for instructions on installing the software necessary to access the information on the CD-ROM. On the CD you'll find:

• All of the Web sites featured in this book. If you *don't* have access to the Internet, you can use the CD to get a taste of what the Web offers. Just select the Local tour and click only on the blue words next to the small yellow "HOT" logo. You'll be able to visit each site in the book and explore three to five links within it. Remember to use the black arrow at the top of the screen to move within the CD's contents. If you *do* have a modem and a SLIP/PPP connection, you can select the Live tour and go onto the Web via the CD.

• *Classroom Connect's* entire Web site, which features links to more than 300 education sites on the Net. You'll also find information about mounting your school's Web pages on the site, plus information about the products we make that help K-12 educators use the Internet in the classroom.

• Several large QuickTime Movie clips of *Classroom Connect's* video, *World Wide Web Revealed*. It's the final tape in our four-tape Internet Revealed series designed to teach teachers and in-service leaders how to use the Internet.

Conventions used

• All Internet addresses are in **bold** type. Names of directories, subdirectories, filenames, and menu items are in *italics*.

• Except for the color section, the letters **URL** are always at the beginning of the address of an Internet site. **Do not** type those letters in when you use your Web browser.

• We've avoided breaking a Web site address whenever possible. When we have to break a particularly long address, we divide it after the slash. See the example below.

> **URL: http://www.cchem.berkeley.edu/**
> **Table/index.html**

• Internet sites not on the Web, such as a gopher site or newsgroup, also begin with the letters URL. You can access those sites via your Web browser by typing in the letters **gopher://**, **ftp://**, etc., followed by the address.

Accuracy of Internet addresses

All sites in this book were verified as close to deadline as possible. But because the Web is an evolving community, the addresses of Web sites often change. If you try an address and can't access or find it, take these steps.

• Check and retype the address.

• You may receive a message saying the site has moved. It will give you the new address, sort of like the post office notifying you of an address change. Be sure to write it down or add it to your bookmarks.

• You could strip the address down to what is called the *root directory* and then try accessing it again. In the following site address, you would delete everything after **edu**. What remains is the root directory, which is the file the Web site information resides in at the computer.

> **URL: http://www.cchem.berkeley.edu/Table/index.html**

• If all else fails, go to the *Classroom Connect* Web site and use one of the six Web searching tools on the Search page to find the site on the Web.

> **URL: http://www.wentworth.com/classroom/search.htm**

What you'll find on a typical page

Each page in this book is devoted to a single site, but features several packages of information. We've dissected a page to help you find what you need quickly.

Name of the chapter/general subject. The specific topic of the site is in parentheses. If the site is a general resource with a huge database, you'll see this general resource icon: ▣.

Name of the site or specific topic.

The site's URL address on the WWW. (Do not type the letters **URL** when typing the address into your browser.)

A "screen capture" showing the home page or a typical page from the site.

A paragraph describing the value of this site as it applies to educators and students.

One or two ideas for ways educators could use this site with their students.

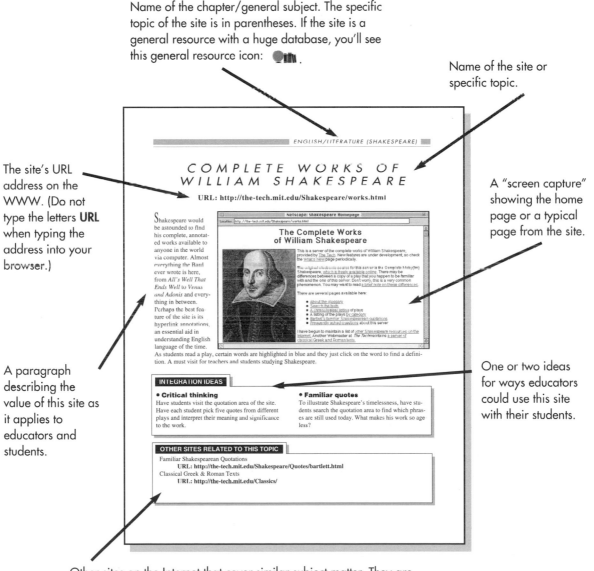

Other sites on the Internet that cover similar subject matter. They are primarily Web sites, but you will also find some gopher sites or newsgroups. These are accessible via URL and your Web browser. If a site is helpful for other subject areas, e.g. history, you'll see the subject in parentheses next to the site name, e.g. (History).

CHAPTER

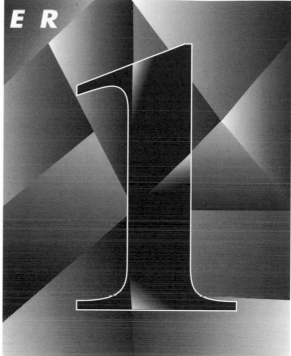

ART

AGE OF ENLIGHTENMENT IN FRANCE

URL: http://dmf.culture.fr/files/imaginary_exhibition.html

Add a colorful, interactive touch to your existing lessons about the Age of Enlightenment in France. Students can learn about this period (1715-1799) by sampling this site's historical background of the time, biographies of artists and selections of their work, and a genealogy of French royalty. Of special note is a detailed description of how art was commissioned during this period.

INTEGRATION IDEA

● **Define patrons**

Have students use this site to do a keyword search on patrons. Have them use their findings to discuss individual and state patronage of the arts and its effects. Have them create a scrapbook of the art and describe the type of patronage involved in each. Discuss modern art patronage, such as the National Endowment for the Arts.

OTHER SITES RELATED TO THIS TOPIC

French Revolution
   URL: http://dmf.culture.fr/files/revolution.html
Painting of General Napoleon Bonaparte
   URL: http://dmf.culture.fr/oeuvres/Gros.gif
French Age of Enlightenment Genealogy (History)
   URL: http://dmf.culture.fr/files/genealogie.html

ANSEL ADAMS: FIAT LUX

URL: http://bookweb.cwis.uci.edu:8042/AdamsHome.html

Plenty of information about this renowned photographer can be found here, including historical and biographical essays. But the real value of this site stems from the hundreds of online photos from the Adams exhibition at the University of California. The site is well-organized and indexed, with thumbnail graphics that give you a preview of each piece. Next to many photos you'll find links to sound clips of Adams discussing the work. This site is a wonderful example of how teachers can take students on virtual tours via the Web's multimedia, interactive capabilities.

INTEGRATION IDEAS

• **Field trip**
As students study Yosemite's influence on Adams, have them think of inspiring natural areas near them. Plan a trip to one so students can photograph or sketch the area.

• **Distant tours**
Discuss the value of being able to tour distant places such as museums and galleries using the Internet.

OTHER SITES RELATED TO THIS TOPIC

Photography Homepage
URL: http://www.mcs.net:80/~rjacobs/home.html
Photography Newsgroups
URL: news:rec.photo.darkroom
URL: news:rec.photo.help
URL: news:rec.photo.advanced

(ART)^N VIRTUAL PHOTOGRAPHY LABORATORY

URL: http://www.artn.nwu.edu

Artists around the world are beginning to use high-end computers and the Internet to create new forms of visual art. This Web site is your students' link to the exhibitions of online artists who use these sophisticated electronic tools to create virtual sculptures, photographs, holograms, and paintings. Each month, a new artist is featured on this site, along with technical notes on how they created their artwork.

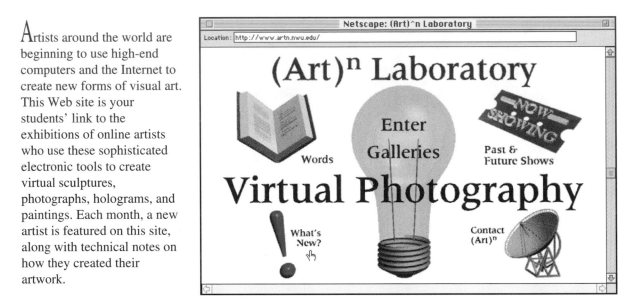

INTEGRATION IDEA

● **Multimedia project**

As students tour the site, have them note how these artists are bringing their work to the public via trade shows, university-sponsored exhibits, galleries, and the Internet. Have them create a multimedia presentation about the various kinds of visual art on the Internet.

OTHER SITES RELATED TO THIS TOPIC

Computer Photography & Graphics Resources
       URL: gopher://siggraph.org
       URL: news:rec.photo.advanced
       URL: news:comp.graphics
       URL: http://mambo.ucsc.edu/psl/cg.html
       URL: http://www-graphics.stanford.edu/demos/

ART HISTORY
VIA ARTSERVE

URL: http://rubens.anu.edu.au/

Four centuries of art, mainly from the Mediterranean region, is at students' fingertips at this server. It offers access to about 10,200 images, a full-length art history book, and a mechanism for searching its data via an interactive interface. You can search by artist, technique, or content. The image collection consists of some 2,800 images of prints, largely from the fifteenth to the end of the nineteenth century, and more than 8,500 images of architecture and architectural sculpture.

INTEGRATION IDEAS

• Study an artist
Have students pick an artist, do a keyword search of the site, and analyze the works for style and content. How did the artist's work evolve over time? Compare an early work to a late one.

• Define propaganda
Have students examine the photos from "Triumph of the Will," a Nazi-oriented film by Leni Riefenstahl, and talk about the power of art as propaganda. What makes these images so powerful?

OTHER SITES RELATED TO THIS TOPIC

Images of Classical, Medieval, and Renaissance Architecture
  URL: http://rubens.anu.edu.au/laserdisk/laserdisk.html
Interactive Database of Historical Architecture
  URL: http://rubens.anu.edu.au/laserdisk/michael/archtrial_form.html
ArtServe Text Search of Historical Documents (History)
  URL: http://rubens.anu.edu.au/searchmenu.html

ASIAN ARTS

URL: http://www.webart.com/asianart/index.html

Asian art provides teachers with a great opportunity to graphically teach world cultures. This site offers a large database of Asian art exhibitions, articles, and online galleries of modern and historical artwork. Currently available are an Early Tibetan Mandalas exhibition, the Peaceful Wind and Traders of the Lost Arts galleries, and results of recent Asian art auctions at Christie's in London.

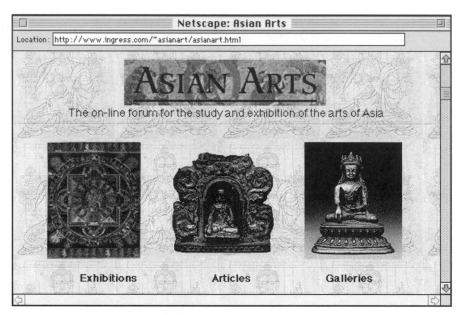

INTEGRATION IDEA

• Art identification
Have students define mandalas (designs symbolic of the universe) and examine those in the Early Tibetan Mandalas exhibit. How were mandalas used by ancient artists? How are modern artists influenced by their work? Present students with a fragment of art (a portion of a photo) and have them determine its period and explain how they derived their answers.
URL: http://www.ingress.com/~asianart/

OTHER SITES RELATED TO THIS TOPIC

Krannert Art Museum Asian Art
URL: http://www.art.uiuc.edu/kam/Guide/Asian/Asian.html
Smithsonian Asian Art Online
URL: http://www.si.edu
Tibetan Sculptures and Paintings
URL: http://www.ingress.com/~asianart/pw/pw1.html

CARLOS' INTERACTIVE COLORING BOOK

URL: http://robot0.ge.uiuc.edu/~carlosp/color/

Your K-3 students will adore this interactive coloring book! Students can pick one of seven black and white images to color in, and then, using a mouse, point and click on the areas they want to color. When finished, they can retrieve a graphic image of their finished work to print out. The available pictures include Birthday, Christmas, Clown, Flower, House, and Snowman.

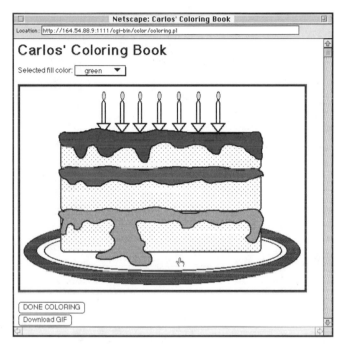

INTEGRATION IDEA

- **Color online**

Have your young art students color in one or more of the images, and then retrieve them for printing. Create a bulletin board of their finished work. Keep in mind that there's an expert coloring book option for more advanced students, and those with slower Internet connections. This gives students more flexibility when coloring in their pictures.

OTHER SITES RELATED TO THIS TOPIC

Christmas Toy Trek Adventure
    URL: http://www.dash.com/netro/fun/ttrek/ttrek.html
Coloring Book Software for Macintosh
    URL: ftp://ftp.wentworth.com/wentworth/Classroom-Connect/Teacher-Aids/coloring-book.hqx
OTIS Art Links for Kids
    URL: http://www.interlog.com/~gordo/kids.htm

FRANK LLOYD WRIGHT ARCHITECTURE EXHIBIT

URL: http://flw.badgernet.com:2080

Frank Lloyd Wright is recognized as one of the twentieth century's greatest architects. His buildings represent some of the world's most important architectural treasures. Students in search of an intimate look at the life and work of Wright will find it in Wisconsin—his birthplace and home for most of his life, as well as here in this new online exhibit. The most impressive Web page on this site features links to photographs of his work.
URL: http://flw.badgernet.com:2080/gallery.htm

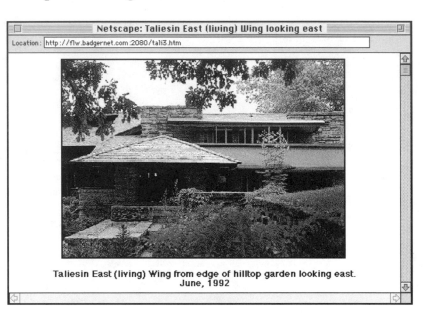

Taliesin East (living) Wing from edge of hilltop garden looking east.
June, 1992

QuickTime videos of interviews with Wright can also be found here.
URL: http://flw.badgernet.com:2080/galndex.htm

INTEGRATION IDEA

• Design a building

Have students study Wright and his work via this site. What do the works tell you about the man? How does his work tie in with nature? How has his work inspired today's architects? Have students design buildings for different geographical conditions (e.g., desert, woodlands) and also design furniture to harmonize with "organic" architecture. Would Wright use architectural design software?

OTHER SITES RELATED TO THIS TOPIC

Frank Lloyd Wright: American Architect
> **URL: http://silver.ucs.indiana.edu/~wschende/frank.html**

Frank Lloyd Wright Biographical Data & Photos
> **URL: http://www.math.uic.edu/oakpark/FLW.html**

Frank Lloyd Wright Wisconsin Tour Guide Online
> **URL: http://flw.badgernet.com:2080/brochure.htm**

GLOBAL SHOW-N-TELL

URL: http://emma.manymedia.com:80/show-n-tell/

Global Show-n-Tell is a virtual exhibition that lets children show off their favorite projects, possessions, accomplishments, and collections to kids (and adults) around the world. Global Show-n-Tell is for kids, it's for fun, and it's free. The exhibition consists of links to children's artwork in the form of multimedia pages residing in World Wide Web or ftp servers. Why not enter your students' work in the Global Show-n-Tell Exhibition? Visit the site to find out how!

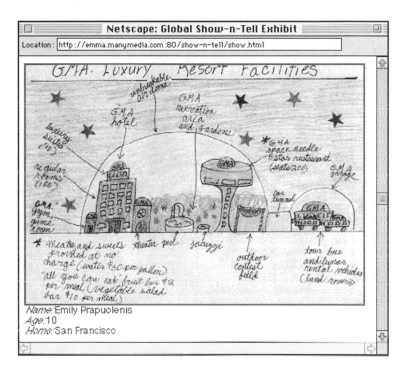

INTEGRATION IDEA

• Put work online

By submitting your students' work to the site, you can introduce them to publishing their work to a worldwide audience using the Internet. After the class completes an assignment, scan in their work and submit it to the site. By itself, having your students merely visit the site is a great way to introduce them to the World Wide Web and to see what other kids are doing online.

OTHER SITES RELATED TO THIS TOPIC

Student Art Work from Alaska
> **URL: http://www.northstar.k12.ak.us/schools/upk/graphics.html**

Kennedy Student Art Gallery
> **URL: http://www.isd77.k12.mn.us/schools/kennedy/openhouse/artgallery.html**

Plugged In
> **URL: http://www.pluggedin.org**

HYPERVISION ONLINE GALLERY

URL: http://www.magic.ca/magicmedia/hypervision.html

HyperVision is an online gallery for aspiring artists looking for a worldwide audience. Current exhibits include "The Night Sky" by Audra Noble, "The Florida Series" by Stephen Stober, and "Electronic Illustrations" by Greg Mably. Visitors are invited to post comments about the artists' work.

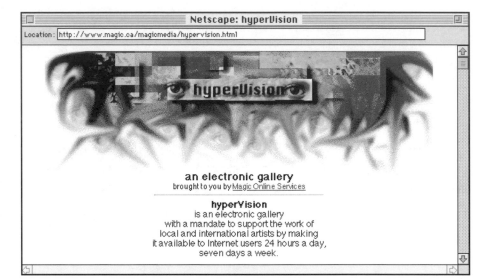

INTEGRATION IDEAS

• Post artwork
Have students visit this site. Then have them post their artwork on your school's World Wide Web server and invite visitors to email or post comments. How does this compare to face-to-face comments artists might receive in a gallery?

• Discuss galleries
Discuss the different ways artwork can be displayed in a gallery, as opposed to an electronic gallery. What types of art are better suited to each and why?

OTHER SITES RELATED TO THIS TOPIC

Adventures on the Right Side of the Brain Online Exhibit
> **URL: http://www-sloan.mit.edu/Gallery/Maruska/maruska.html**

Art Space: Online Art Exhibit by and for High School Students
> **URL: http://superdec.uni.uiuc.edu/departments/finearts/art/artspace/uniartspace.html**

Online Art Exhibits at Rice University
> **URL: http://riceinfo.rice.edu/Exhibits/**

LEONARDO DA VINCI MUSEUM

URL: http://leonardo.net/gallery.html#start

The original "Renaissance Man," Leonardo da Vinci was a great painter, designer, scientist, futurist, and thinker. His works are more popular now than they were in his day. This online museum is divided into several wings: East Wing: Oil Paintings including "Mona Lisa" and "The Last Supper"; West Wing: Engineering and Futuristic Designs, including fantastic weapons and several flying machines; North Wing: Drawings and Sketches, including illustrations, anatomical sketches, and unfinished works; and South Wing: Life and Times of Leonardo da Vinci, a historical exhibit.

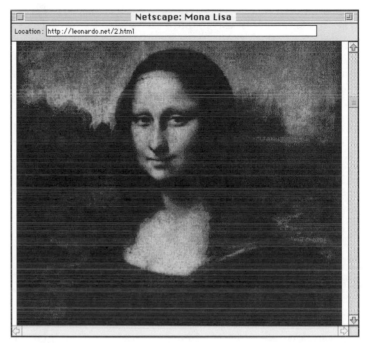

Netscape: Mona Lisa
Location: http://leonardo.net/2.html

INTEGRATION IDEA

• Make a machine
Have students peruse this exhibit and record which of da Vinci's machines, designs, ideas, etc., have influenced modern designs and machines, e.g., helicopter, submarine. Have them draw, and perhaps even make, machines of their own out of toothpicks, popsicle sticks, etc.

OTHER SITES RELATED TO THIS TOPIC

The Louvre Online Leonardo da Vinci Exhibit
    URL: http://www.cnam.fr/louvre/paint/auth/vinci/index.html
Leonardo da Vinci Images
    URL: http://sop.geo.umn.edu/~reudi/leonardo.html
History of Mathematics: Leonardo da Vinci (Mathematics)
    URL: http://aleph0.clarku.edu/~djoyce/mathhist/chronology.html

LITE-BRITE

URL: http://www.galcit.caltech.edu/~ta/lb/lb.html

This is a fun, colorful way to introduce younger students to the World Wide Web. Older students will remember their childhood days using the real-world version of the Lite-Brite toy, pushing colorful, translucent pegs into lighted boxes to create pictures. Now, art students around the world can create their own works of Lite-Brite art online!

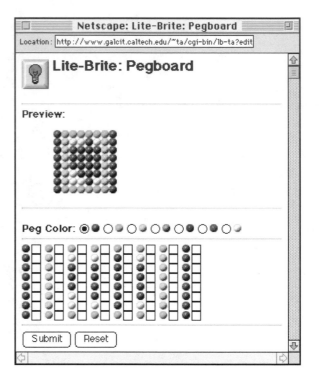

INTEGRATION IDEA

• Create a picture

Have students spend a class period creating their own work of art using this site. When they're done, allow them to send their work to the site itself, which organizers will add to the growing database of work. A variation on this idea is to break the class into four to five groups and collaborate on a larger Lite-Brite project. Special needs students will find this site especially rewarding and fun!

OTHER SITES RELATED TO THIS TOPIC

Legos
      URL: http://legowww.homepages.com
Mr. Potato Head
      URL: http://winnie.acsu.buffalo.edu/cgi-bin/potato
Scratch Pad
      URL: http://american.recordings.com/WWWoM/cgi-bin/SP/

THE LOUVRE

URL: http://mistral.enst.fr/~pioch/louvre/louvre.shtml

This version of the Musee du Louvre, perhaps the most famous art museum in the world, is free and open to the public 24 hours a day! Visit the famous painting exhibition (from Cezanne to Picasso), the Louvre's Auditorium, and a medieval art exhibit. (Note the "mirror sites" listed below. Your connection will be much faster if you access a site close to you rather than the main address in Paris.) Students can also take a short tour of Paris through the site.
URL: http://sunsite.unc.edu/ wm/paris/

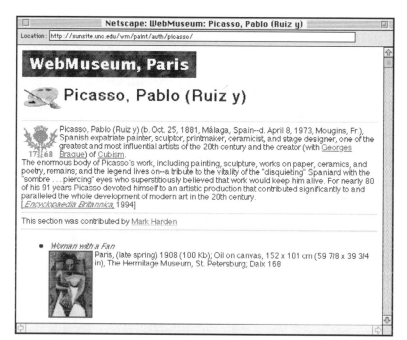

INTEGRATION IDEAS

• Light and color
While touring the site, have students find examples of Cubism and Impressionism and compare artists' use of light and color. How do these works relate to modern art? What influence did Cezanne have on Cubism?

• Art search
If students are new to art history, simply allow them to browse this site. They'll be surprised at how many works are instantly familiar to them, e.g., Mona Lisa.

OTHER SITES RELATED TO THIS TOPIC

The Louvre Mirror Site in North Carolina
> **URL: http://sunsite.unc.edu/louvre/**

The Louvre Mirror Site in Florida
> **URL: http://www.oir.ucf.edu/louvre/**

The Louvre Mirror Site in Australia
> **URL: http://cutl.city.unisa.edu.au/louvre/**

ORIGAMI PAGE

URL: http://www.cs.ubc.ca/spider/jwu/origami.html

Your art students will love visiting this site to learn more about the art of origami! More than three dozen printable origami designs are featured here. Origami has been practiced for hundreds of years in Japan, where its use ranges from the religious (specially-folded pieces of paper adorn many objects in Shinto rituals, and many offerings are wrapped in paper folded in certain prescribed ways) to the traditional, keep-the-kids-occupied-on-a-rainy-day activity.

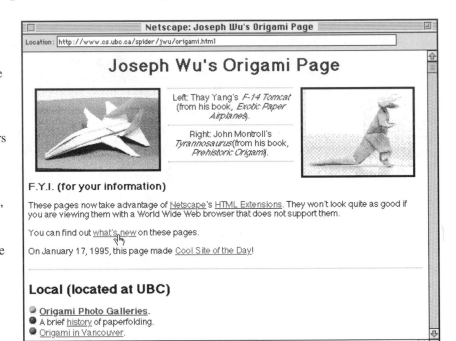

Netscape: Joseph Wu's Origami Page

Location: http://www.cs.ubc.ca/spider/jwu/origami.html

Joseph Wu's Origami Page

Left: Thay Yang's *F-14 Tomcat* (from his book, *Erotic Paper Airplanes*).

Right: John Montroll's *Tyrannosaurus* (from his book, *Prehistoric Origami*).

F.Y.I. (for your information)

These pages now take advantage of Netscape's HTML Extensions. They won't look quite as good if you are viewing them with a World Wide Web browser that does not support them.

You can find out what's new on these pages.

On January 17, 1995, this page made Cool Site of the Day!

Local (located at UBC)

- Origami Photo Galleries.
- A brief history of paperfolding.
- Origami in Vancouver.

INTEGRATION IDEAS

• Comparison study

Have students examine old and new origami designs and composition and paper choices. How is the history of papermaking related to the spread of origami outside Japan?

• Make origami

Have students access this site and download an origami design. Then, have them print it and actually fold the paper according to the instructions.

OTHER SITES RELATED TO THIS TOPIC

How to Fold a Paper Crane
    URL:http://www.mit.edu:8001/people/baspitz/Origami/origami.html
Origami Tips and Links
    URL: http://panther.gsu.edu/~gs01yyj/origami/origami.html
Step-by-Step Paper Folding Project
    URL: http://www.sgi.com:80/grafica/fold/page001.html

OTIS ONLINE ART ARCHIVES

URL: http://sunsite.unc.edu/otis/

OTIS is a place for image-makers and image-lovers to exchange ideas, collaborate and, in a loose sense of the word, meet. Young artists, many of them college students, have Web pages that include autobiographies, examples of their work, and their comments on the pieces shown. (Be aware that nudes can be found at this site.) They invite email comments. Artists young and old can add to OTIS's image collection

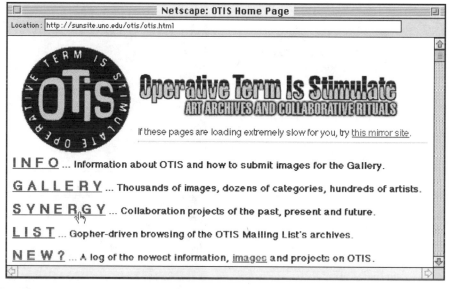

by submitting their own works. For more information, send email to Ed Stastny at **ed@art.net**.

INTEGRATION IDEAS

● **Post artwork**
Have advanced art students submit works as a group or individually to OTIS. Send email to Ed Stastny to learn how to do this.

● **Art project**
Have students use graphic arts software to submit a portion of a graphic to an ongoing, collaborative art project at OTIS. The piece changes as submissions are added. Talk about this type of art and how it compares to traditional art presentation.

OTHER SITES RELATED TO THIS TOPIC

Off the Wall Gallery
   URL: http://nearnet.gnn.com/gnn/mag/gallery/art.html
Ranjit's Art Playground
   URL: http://oz.sas.upenn.edu/gallery/gallery.html
The Electric Art Gallery
   URL: http://www.egallery.com/egallery/homepage.html

SISTINE CHAPEL

URL: http://www.christusrex.org/www1/sistine/0-Tour.html

Built between 1475 and 1483 in the time of Pope Sixtus IV della Rovere, the Sistine Chapel originally served as Palatine Chapel. The chapel is rectangular in shape and measures 40.93 meters long by 13.41 meters wide—the exact dimensions of the Temple of Solomon, as given in the Old Testament. This Web site contains more than 325 images of the chapel, many of them divided by artist or by which portion of the Bible or of the life of Christ is depicted. A master plan for the chapel and the artwork inside helps viewers understand where each piece appears. It can be found at the following location.
URL: http://www.christusrex.org/www1/sistine/0-Plan.jpg

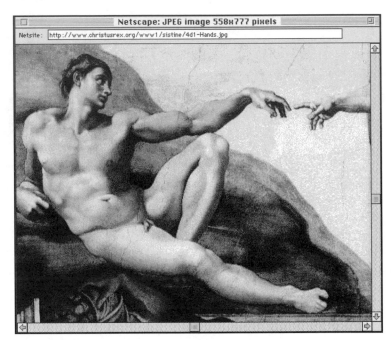

INTEGRATION IDEA

• **Religion and art**
Have students look closely at how the paintings depict Bible stories and the life of Christ. How does the work make the viewer feel about Christianity, religion, and God? Put yourself in the place of someone who is not familiar with the Bible and think about what the art is trying to convey or teach. How have artists around the world used art for religious purposes, or been inspired by the spiritual? Look for examples on the Internet.

OTHER SITES RELATED TO THIS TOPIC

Medieval Resources on the Web
URL: http://athena.english.vt.edu/medieval.html
Vatican City Online
URL: http://www.christusrex.org/www1/citta/0-Citta.html
Christian Internet Resources (Social Sciences/Humanities)
URL: http://hercules.geology.uiuc.edu/~schimmri/christianity/christian.html

VIRTUAL ART STUDY TOUR

URL: http://archpropplan.auckland.ac.nz/misc/virtual_tour.html

Walk like an Egyptian around the palace of Ramses III! This architectural site gives students the ability to "walk through" computer reproductions of ancient buildings and modern structures, even one by Mies van der Rohe. Students click on direction buttons to move through the buildings as if they were walking through them. A very hands-on, fun way to introduce them to the next generation in Internet navigation!

INTEGRATION IDEAS

• Make a model

After students research and tour one of the buildings at the site, have them construct a three-dimensional model of the structure. What does the hands-on experience of building a model teach them about architecture and design?

• Architectural software

If design software is available, have students design a building so viewers can virtually "walk" through the structure.

OTHER SITES RELATED TO THIS TOPIC

Architectural Tours Online
URL: http://archpropplan.auckland.ac.nz/People/Mat/gallery/gallery.html
University of Auckland, New Zealand Virtual Tour
URL: http://www.auckland.ac.nz/arch/movies/tiflight.mpg

C H A P T R

B U S I N E S S

19

AMERICAN ACCOUNTING ASSOCIATION

URL: http://www.rutgers.edu/Accounting/raw/aaa/aaa.htm

Bring the real world of accounting to your students with the AAA's Web site. It has links to a growing database of case studies involving real-world accounting situations, as well as dozens of links to accounting-related online sites around the world. Here's an excerpt from an online case study involving "phantom profits" at Cineplex Odeon: "On May 29, 1989 *Forbes* ran an article on Cineplex Odeon based upon the detective work of a group of accountants in Los Angeles who specialize in exposing dubious accounting practices. The report stated that the company's

reported $44 million gain should have been a $41 million loss. Assume you are a new financial analyst with an investment management company. Your supervisor has asked you to prepare an independent report on the current profitability of Cineplex Odeon so that the appropriate recommendation can be made to your clients."

INTEGRATION IDEA

• **Ethics study**
Use the case studies at the site to spur student discussion of business ethics and accounting practices.
URL: http://www.rutgers.edu/Accounting/raw/aaa/teach/cases.htm

---

OTHER SITES RELATED TO THIS TOPIC

Accounting Resources on the Internet
   URL: http://www.rutgers.edu/Accounting/raw/internet/internet.htm
Ernst & Young Online
   URL: http://www.worldserver.pipex.com/ernsty/
The Accounting Network (ANet)
   URL: gopher://elli.scu.edu:70/00/anet/journals/intro

BUSINESS SCHOOLS ON THE INTERNET

URL: http://www.yahoo.com/Business/Business_Schools/

Students need not pile into the car to check out college campuses. This site links them to more than 250 business schools with Web presences on the Internet. Any student interested in studying business in college can use this site to research prospective schools, their campuses, tuition costs, scholarship availability, and course offerings.

INTEGRATION IDEA

• Comparison study

Have students research possible higher education opportunities using the data at the site. Have them compare and contrast the offerings of each school, including cost and scholarship availability.

OTHER SITES RELATED TO THIS TOPIC

Harvard Business School
> **URL: http://rigel.hbs.harvard.edu**

U.S. & Foreign Business School Listing
> **URL: http://riskweb.bus.utexas.edu/bschool.html**

Wharton School of the University of Pennsylvania
> **URL: http://www.wharton.upenn.edu**

BUSINESS SITES INDEX VIA THE MBA PAGE

URL: http://www.cob.ohio-state.edu/dept/fin/mba.htm

Set up as a guide to help MBA students "survive and thrive," this Web site also serves as a unique, comprehensive index to Internet sites of interest to business students at any level. It features links to tips and tricks for getting into business school, MBA Survival and News pages, class and case study materials, tips on how to find a job, online resume

services, MBA placement statistics, and MBA program rankings for U.S. business schools.

INTEGRATION IDEAS

• Assess programs

Have students access MBA programs' data on placement of graduates and their salaries. Have them compare the programs to learn which programs offer the best value for the tuition dollar.

• Online resumes

Have students access the online resumes and critique them for content and presentation. Have them design an online resume and note the differences between an online resume and a traditional one.

OTHER SITES RELATED TO THIS TOPIC

Corporate Annual Reports Online
    URL: http://www.yahoo.com/Economy/Markets_and_Investments/Corporate_Reports/
Financial Economic Network's Virtual Business School
    URL: http://www.clemson.edu/~marrm/school.html
Hoover's Ultimate Source of Business Information Online
    URL: http://www.hoovers.com/HOnline.html

D I G I C A S H

URL: http://www.digicash.com

It's the hottest topic on the Internet—digital cash. How should it be created, distributed, and used? What about security? The answer to these questions is DigiCash. You use your credit card number to buy credits to purchase online merchandise. A visit to the site shows students first-hand how the online marketplace is developing and they can explore the next generation of financial transactions.

INTEGRATION IDEAS

• Electronic money
Have students access the site and write their impressions of DigiCash and other online payment systems. (See below.) Are they feasible prototypes? What improvements and uses can students suggest?

• Evolution of money
Have students examine how money has evolved in human societies, working from barter transactions, to the use of shells or other objects, to government production of coins and paper bills. How important is currency to a nation state? Is electronic currency "state-less"?

OTHER SITES RELATED TO THIS TOPIC

CAFE Electronic Wallet
> **URL: http://www.digicash.com/products/projects/cafe.html**

CheckFree Electronic Payment Service
> **URL: http://www.checkfree.com**

Mondex Electronic Smart Cards
> **URL: http://www.mondex.com/mondex/home.htm**

GLOBAL CURRENCY CONVERTER

URL: http://gnn.com/cgi-bin/gnn/currency

For a great exercise in global currency, take students to this Web site to illustrate global currencies and their fluid nature. This site acts as an online, real-time currency converter. Just select a currency from the list, such as the German mark, and all other currencies listed will be converted relative to the one you selected.

> **Netscape: The GNN/Koblas Currency Converter**
>
> Location: http://gnn.com/cgi-bin/gnn/currency
>
> ## The Global Network Navigator/Koblas Currency Converter
>
> *by David Koblas*
>
> Using the **Koblas Currency Converter** is very simple. Just select the desired currency and all other currencies will be converted relative to the one you selected. The name of the currency will also appear just below this message.
>
> **This week's currency rates (one US dollar equals)**
>
> *Updated weekly--last 11 May 1995*
>
> | | |
> |---|---|
> | Argentina: | 1.0000 |
> | Australia: | 1.3748 |
> | Austria: | 9.7700 |
> | Belgium: | 28.490 |
> | Brazil: | 0.90000 |
> | Britain: | 0.63060 |
> | Canada: | 1.3535 |
> | Chile: | 372.45 |
> | China: | 8.3064 |
> | Colombia: | 879.80 |
> | Czech Republic: | 25.750 |
> | Denmark: | 5.4230 |
> | ECU: | 0.75180 |

INTEGRATION IDEAS

• Current events

Have students track an individual currency, such as the dollar or the yen, over the course of several weeks or months. At the same time, have them track current events in the world and in the nation. Have them interpret the data, linking the ups and downs of the currency's value to news events.

• Math exercise

As a math exercise, have students access currency values for the mark, the yen, the peso, and the pound and work out how many dollars they would receive in a one-to-one exchange. They can check their answers using this site.

OTHER SITES RELATED TO THIS TOPIC

Federal Reserve Board Data
> **URL: http://town.hall.org/govt/govt.html**

International Business Practices Guide
> **URL: gopher://UMSLVMA.UMSL.EDU:70/11/LIBRARY/GOVDOCS/IBPA**

Monetary Statistics & Current Economic Conditions
> **URL: gopher://una.hh.lib.umich.edu:70/11/socsci/econ**

INDEX TO COMMERCIAL SITES ON THE INTERNET

URL: http://www.directory.net/

More and more businesses are going online everyday. This single Web site is your link to those businesses—more than 5,000 at last count! These links will be of particular interest to high school business students studying the latest business trends and new ways of doing business—namely via the Internet and other online services. A list of more than 50 other online business site indexes can also be found on the site at the following address. **URL: http://www.directory.net/dir/indexes.html**

> **Netscape: Commercial Services on the Net**
> Location: http://www.directory.net/dir/directory.html
>
> # Commercial Services on the Net
>
> These pages list the entries in **Open Market's** Commercial Sites Index.
>
> Enter a word or two that describes what you are looking for:
>
> [Aerospace] [Search]
>
> See also:
> - What's New
> - How to submit listings
> - Send us your feedback!
>
> ## Business and Commercial
>
> There are **4601** listings in this category. You can browse all listings for this category, or select a letter to move to that section:
>
> A B C D E F G H I J K L M N O P Q R S T U V W X Y Z

INTEGRATION IDEA

• Keyword search

Have each student pick an industry or business, such as travel, and then logon to the site. Instruct them to do a keyword search for the business and keep a detailed journal of the sites they visit. Which types of businesses use the Internet most, and how? Why does Net use seem more conducive to some industries and businesses than others?

OTHER SITES RELATED TO THIS TOPIC

BizWeb
    URL: http://www.bizweb.com
Canadian Business Directory
    URL: http://cibd.com/cibd/
Virtual Yellow Pages
    URL: http://www.imsworld.com/yp/

INTER@CTIVE WEEK

URL: http://www.zdnet.com/~intweek/

*I*nter@ctive Week is one of the newest, most comprehensive weekly magazines devoted to covering the online and multimedia business world. Each week, the entire issue is posted to this Web site, containing dozens

of top stories, quotes of the week, commentary, features focusing on electronic commerce, media, advertising, and telecommunications in general, stories about regulation, legislation, and policy issues, and general finance news and views.

INTEGRATION IDEA

• Media online
Have students regularly access the site to read the publication as part of your current events or business curriculum. Do they enjoy reading magazines this way? Have them compare the online reading experience to traditional magazine reading. What are the advantages and disadvantages? Do they think print publications will become extinct? What does this mean for the print, publishing, and newspaper industries?

OTHER SITES RELATED TO THIS TOPIC

Business Week
  URL: http://www.enews.com/magazines/bw/
National Public Radio (NPR)
  URL: http://www.npr.org
The Economist
  URL: http://www.enews.com/magazines/economist/

INTERNAL REVENUE SERVICE (IRS)

URL: http://www.ustreas.gov/treasury/bureaus/irs/irs.html

The taxman is online, with a purpose. The mission of the Internal Revenue Service is to collect the proper amount of tax revenue at the least cost to the public in a manner warranting the highest degree of public confidence in its integrity, efficiency, and fairness. Thus, "Our presence on the Internet and the World-Wide Web is part of our continuing efforts to provide broad and immediate electronic access to IRS tax information, forms, and services. You should view this effort as a work-in-progress."

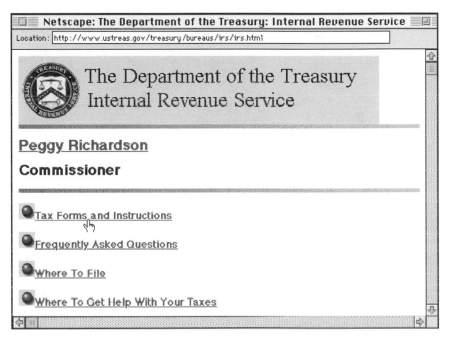

INTEGRATION IDEA

● **Complete a tax form**
Prepare students for life with taxes by having them access this site, retrieve tax forms, and print them for use in class. Teach them how to fill out a basic 1040 and a more difficult business tax form. Address the possibilities of electronic filing.

OTHER SITES RELATED TO THIS TOPIC

State Tax Forms & Information
    URL: http://www.scubed.com:8001/tax/state/state_index.html
Taxing Times
    URL: http://www.scubed.com:8001/tax/tax.html
Tax Software
    URL: ftp://ftp.scubed.com/pub/proffer/tax/

INTERNET MARKETING ARCHIVES

URL: http://galaxy.einet.net:80/hypermail/inet-marketing/

The practice of marketing on the Internet is controversial and has generated much debate. The Internet Marketing online mailing list was established to discuss the appropriate marketing of services, ideas, and items to and on the Internet. More than 3,000 people and sites involved in all aspects of marketing, sales, programming, journalism, and other fields actively participate in this forum. This list is a good

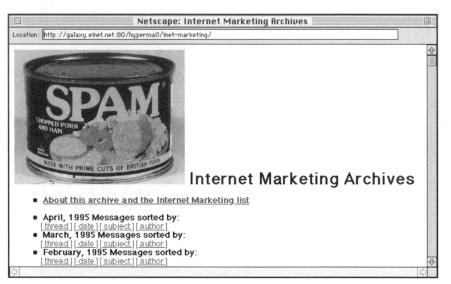

source for people who want to create Internet sites, market products and goods in appropriate ways, develop payment systems, or write about what's going on. This Web site acts as a storehouse for all current and past posts to the list, and is an excellent research tool for students studying online marketing and sales.

INTEGRATION IDEAS

● Product marketing
Have students access this site to keep up to date on issues and success stories concerning online commerce. Have them think of a product or service and design a plan for marketing it via the Internet. Junior Achievement participants could actually market their products online.

● Personal marketing
Have students brainstorm the different ways they could use the Internet to market themselves, via Web pages, mailing lists, etc. What does it mean for a person to have a "Net presence"?

OTHER SITES RELATED TO THIS TOPIC

Clueless Marketing on the Internet
      URL: http://worcester.lm.com:80/lmann/clueless.html
Internet Advertiser Blacklist
      URL: http://math-www.uni-paderborn.de:80/~axel/blacklist.html
SuperBusinessNET
      URL: http://www.sbusiness.com

MORTGAGE CALCULATOR

URL: http://ibc.wustl.edu/mort.html

Buying a house is probably the biggest investment a person makes in a lifetime. Bring your students to this site to teach them the terms and money issues that come with home ownership. The site features an online mortgage calculator you can use to input the principal loan balance, annual interest rate, amortization length, and the monthly

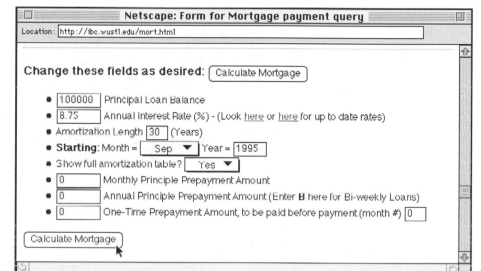

prepayment amount. The computer sends detailed mortgage payment information back to you. A very slick, easy-to-use site with great classroom applications.

INTEGRATION IDEA

• Financial planning
Have students play the role of home buyer and go through the entire process of buying a home, from finding one in their price range to closing the sale. They can use this site to calculate the size of the mortgage they can afford.

OTHER SITES RELATED TO THIS TOPIC

Homebuyers Fair
    URL: http://www.homefair.com
HomeNet
    URL: http://www.intertel.com
RealtyLinks Home Page
    URL: http://www.xmission.com/~realtor1/

29

NETWORTH PERSONAL INVESTING ONLINE

URL: http://networth.galt.com/www/home/insider/insider.htm

Students can be their own stockbrokers with this Web site featuring links to hundreds of free, online resources pertaining to individual investing. Price quotes and charts, ticker information, mutual funds,

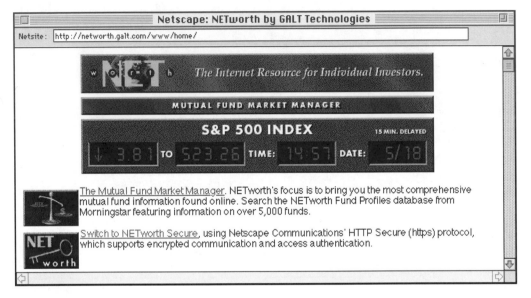

stocks, bonds, public companies, and portfolio, tax, insurance, and currency and exchange rate tracking services make NETworth a must visit for all business students.

INTEGRATION IDEAS

● Stock game

Have students use this site to create their own simulated personal investment portfolio, starting with $100,000 in funny money. Have them track their portfolios for a year and see whose investments return the most.

● Comparison study

Divide students into groups and give each a different type of investment to research and track, e.g., municipal bonds, stocks, mutual funds, and U.S. Treasury bills. Have them report on their performance and talk about the pluses and minuses of the type of investment.

OTHER SITES RELATED TO THIS TOPIC

FinanceHub
> **URL: http://www.catalog.com:80/intersof/**

GNN Personal Investment Center
> **URL: http://gnn.com/gnn/meta/finance/index.html**

FINWeb
> **URL: http://finweb.bus.utexas.edu/finweb.html**

PAWWS: WALL STREET ON THE INTERNET

URL: http://pawws.secapl.com

For up-to-the-minute stock information, this should be students' first stop. This site helps them learn to use the Internet to learn about the stock market, finance, industry, and trade. The Quote Server provides the latest Dow Jones and securities market information and lets you enter stock symbols to get daily updates. Click the Financial Library button to jump to a whole page of links to business and finance resources on the Net.

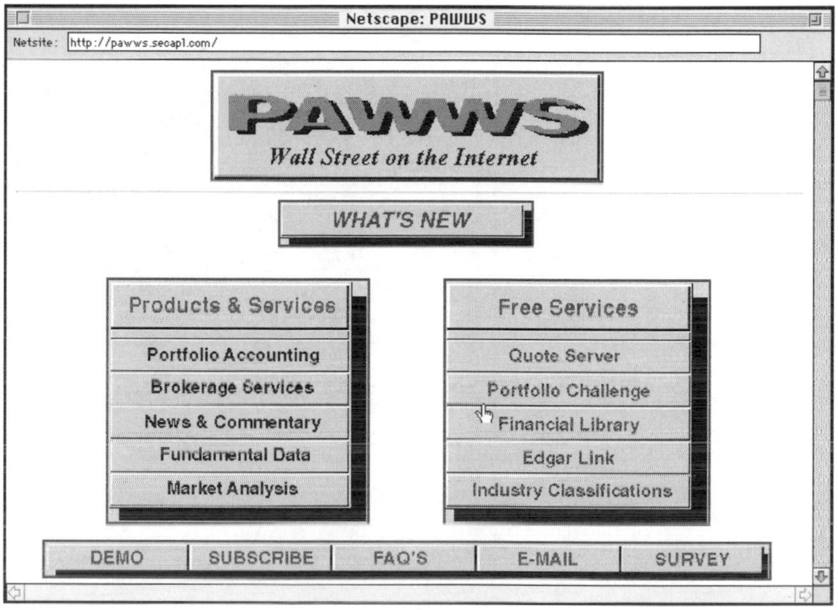

INTEGRATION IDEAS

• Simulation

Have students compete in the PAWWS Portfolio Management Challenge, an online stock market simulation. **URL: http://pawws.secapl.com/ G_phtml/help/help.html**

• Business information

Ask students to compare "traditional" sources of business information, such as newspapers or television, with online sources. Are there advantages to using the Internet to track business interests?

OTHER SITES RELATED TO THIS TOPIC

EDGAR Database
    URL: http://town.hall.org/edgar/edgar.html
Experimental Stock Market Data
    URL: http://www.ai.mit.edu/stocks.html
Quote.Com Stock Quote Server
    URL: http://www.quote.com

W O R L D   B A N K

URL: http://www.worldbank.org

The story of the World Bank is a fascinating one and will be of tremendous interest to business students with global interests. The bank's mission is to help developing countries reduce poverty and promote sustainable development. In that sense, its goals are similar to those of many governments' development assistance programs. But unlike such aid programs, the World Bank doesn't make grants. It lends

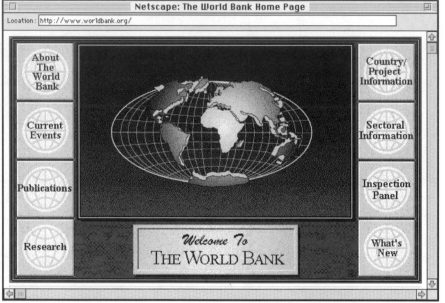

money to developing countries, who repay the loans. Developing countries borrow from the Bank because they need capital, technical assistance, and policy advice.

INTEGRATION IDEA

• Commodities prices

Access the World Bank's "Pink Sheet," its comparison of commodity prices around the world. (Click on What's New and look for the Commodity Policy and Analysis Unit.) Students can pick a commodity, such as rice, and compare its cost in low- and middle-income countries to high-income countries. How does the cost of a commodity affect a nation's economy?

OTHER SITES RELATED TO THIS TOPIC

Banks of the World
URL: http://www.wiso.gwdg.de/ifbg/banking.html
Economic Online Journals
URL: http://www.hkkk.fi/~tormaleh/journals.html
World Bank Publications
URL: http://www.worldbank.org/html/extpb/Publications.html

E N G L I S H /
L I T E R A T U R E

- Bartlett's Familiar Quotations

- British Poetry (1780-1910)

- Children's Literature Web Guide

- Complete Works of William Shakespeare

- Concertina Children's Publisher

- E-Zine-List

- Galaxy's Index of

  English/Literature Resources

- Global Student News

- Myths and Legends

- The Poetry Corner

- Project Gutenberg

- Purdue On-Line Writing Laboratory

- Teaching the American Literatures Archive

BARTLETT'S FAMILIAR QUOTATIONS

URL: http://www.columbia.edu/~svl2/

Want to know who said it when? Students will find the complete, unabridged, and, best of all, searchable database of the ninth edition of Bartlett's Familiar Quotations. In the real world, this book weighs in at more than 1,100-plus pages. The online version's greatest strength is that students can search it by keyword and find quotes from authors such as Geoffrey Chaucer, Sir Walter Raleigh, William Shakespeare, Francis Bacon, Thomas Hobbes, John Milton, Jonathan Swift, John Byron, Thomas Paine, John Quincy Adams, Sir Walter Scott, and Lord Byron.

INTEGRATION IDEAS

• Keyword search
Have students pick a topic such as politics or love and do a keyword search to report on what ten great authors have written on the topic. Which statements do they agree or disagree with, and why?

• Quotable quotes
Have students pick an author and search this database to learn which authors are the most "quotable." What makes a good quote? Have students write their own "quotable quotes."

OTHER SITES RELATED TO THIS TOPIC

Roget's Thesaurus Online
    URL: http://www.neuro.fsu.edu/thesarus.htm
    URL: http://www.notredame.ac.jp/Roget/data/about.html
Webster Dictionary Online
    URL: http://www.cm.cf.ac.uk/dictionaries.html
    URL: http://www.nr.no/ordbok/engelsk/

BRITISH POETRY
(1780-1910)

URL: http://www.lib.virginia.edu/etext/britpo/britpo.html

Students meeting the Romantic poets such as Keats and Byron can learn about the men behind the words at this Web site. It houses a growing library of Romantic and Victorian poetry produced between 1780 and 1910 by British authors. Here's a sampling of some of the works you'll find: John Milton, *Paradise Lost*; Lewis Carroll, *The Hunting of the Snark*; Mary Robinson, *Sappho and Phaon*; Alfred Lord Tennyson, *Charge of the Light Brigade*; and John

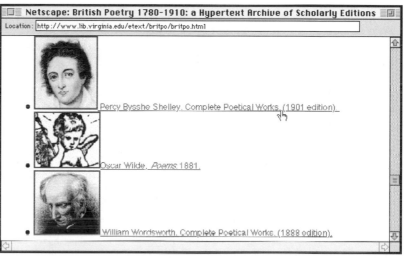

Keats, *The Poetical Works*. Of even greater value are the biographical sources, such as a hyperlinked timeline of Samuel Taylor Coleridge's life, and a dictionary of late eighteenth and early nineteenth century English

INTEGRATION IDEAS

• Timeline

Assign students studying Coleridge to walk through the hyperlinked timeline of his life and other biographical information at the site. Have them report on the life of the man some called a failed genius.

• Compare and contrast

Have students compare the biographical information about Coleridge to that of Shelley at the site. What was different or the same about the men? Give them unidentified passages from their work and ask them to tell you which author wrote the piece. How did they know?

OTHER SITES RELATED TO THIS TOPIC

Nineteenth Century Anglo-Saxon Poetry Database
URL: http://etext.virginia.edu/epd.html
Electronic Text Center
URL: http://www.lib.virginia.edu/etext/ETC.html

CHILDREN'S LITERATURE WEB GUIDE

URL: http://www.ucalgary.ca/~dkbrown/index.html

If you're looking for good children's literature—no matter what the grade level—don't pass by this Web site. Categories in the site's List of Recommended Books include Best Books For Young Adults 1995 (selected by the American Library Association); Books for Young Adult Reluctant Readers; and Sure-fire Can't Miss Books for Junior High Students. Other materials include the full text of dozens of popular children's books and online resources that help parents teach children to read and use the library. The site also includes links to author-specific resources, including

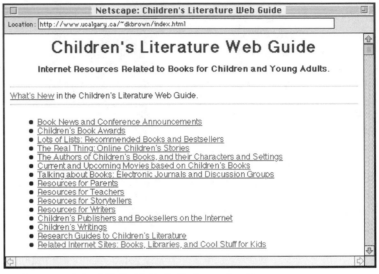

The Lewis Carroll Home Page, the Dr. Seuss Page, and the J.R.R. Tolkein Information Page.

INTEGRATION IDEA

• Post a story
As K-5 students read several children's books, instruct them to think about a topic for a book they'd like to write. Have them write and illustrate their own story and submit it to this site for posting in the Children's Writings area.
URL: http://www.ucalgary.ca/~dkbrown/writings.html
URL: http://en-garde.com/kidpub/intro.html

OTHER SITES RELATED TO THIS TOPIC

Learning to Read
    URL: http://www.ucalgary.ca/~dkbrown/rparent.html
    URL: http://www.ed.gov/pubs/parents/Reading/index.html
Science Fiction Resources
    URL: http://sundry.hsc.usc.edu/hazel/www/sf-resource.guide.html
Writings by Young People
    URL: http://www.ucalgary.ca/~dkbrown/writings.html
World Myths
    URL: http://www.the-wire.com/culture/mythology/mythtext.html

COMPLETE WORKS OF WILLIAM SHAKESPEARE

URL: http://the-tech.mit.edu/Shakespeare/works.html

Shakespeare would be astounded to find his complete, annotated works available to anyone in the world via computer. Almost everything the Bard ever wrote is here, from *All's Well That Ends Well* to *Venus and Adonis* and everything in between. Perhaps the best feature of the site is its hyperlink annotations, an essential aid in

Netscape: Shakespeare Homepage

Location: http://the-tech.mit.edu/Shakespeare/works.html

The Complete Works of William Shakespeare

This is a server of the complete works of William Shakespeare, provided by The Tech. New features are under development, so check the What's New page periodically.

The original electronic source for this server is the Complete Moby(tm) Shakespeare, which is freely available online. There may be differences between a copy of a play that you happen to be familiar with and the one of this server. Don't worry, this is a very common phenomenon. You may want to read a brief note on these differences.

There are several pages available here:

- About the glossary
- Search the texts
- A chronological listing of plays
- A listing of the plays by category
- Bartlett's familiar Shakespearean quotations
- Frequently asked questions about this server

I have begun to maintain a list of other Shakespeare resources on the Internet. Another Webmaster at *The Tech* maintains a server of classical Greek and Roman texts.

understanding English language of the time. As students read a play, certain words are highlighted in blue and they just click on the word to find a definition. A must visit for teachers and students studying Shakespeare.

INTEGRATION IDEAS

• Critical thinking

Have students visit the quotation area of the site. Have each student pick five quotes from different plays and interpret their meaning and significance to the work.

• Familiar quotes

To illustrate Shakespeare's timelessness, have students search the quotation area to find which phrases are still used today. What makes his work so ageless?

OTHER SITES RELATED TO THIS TOPIC

Familiar Shakespearean Quotations
URL: http://the-tech.mit.edu/Shakespeare/Quotes/bartlett.html
Classical Greek & Roman Texts
URL: http://the-tech.mit.edu/Classics/

CONCERTINA CHILDREN'S BOOK PUBLISHER

URL: http://www.digimark.net/iatech/books/intro.htm

Designed for browsing by younger students, Concertina, a Canada-based children's book publisher, has put several of its products online. Each book has been brought online in its entirety, complete with full-color images of every page! This site is a worthwhile visit for all English and literature teachers who want to introduce their students to online reading and publishing. Your students will enjoy clicking through these books, all written for K-2 graders.

INTEGRATION IDEA

● Reading on the Web

Have your students access this site and read one of the stories. Sit with them as they click through a story, and have them compare the experience with reading a real book. Did they like to read it on the computer?

OTHER SITES RELATED TO THIS TOPIC

Children's Stories from England
> URL: http://www.comlab.ox.ac.uk/oucl/users/jonathan.bowen/children.html

InkSpot Resource for Children's Writers
> URL: http://www.interlog.com/~ohi/dmo-pages/writers.html

Newberry Award Winning Books
> URL: http://dab.psi.net/ChapterOne/children/index.html

E - Z I N E - L I S T

URL: http://www.meer.net/~johnl/e-zine-list/index.html

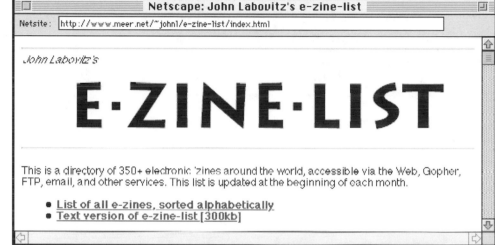

In more than a decade, the Internet has become printing press and home to several hundred electronic magazines, called "ezines" or just "zines" for short. Zines are generally produced by one person or a small group of people, often for fun or personal reasons, and tend to be irreverent and/or esoteric. However, many have applications to English courses of all kinds, and this site contains a list of how to obtain/subscribe to every zine in existence. Here are just a few of the titles of the more popular, applicable zines: *Apokalypso, Attack Poetry, CyberKind, The Elm,* and *InterFace Magazine.*

INTEGRATION IDEA

● Subscribe to a zine

Have each student subscribe to a zine (after you've gone through the list and pulled out the appropriate ones) at the beginning of the school year. Have them read it throughout the year and, during the holiday break or at the end of the year, write an in-depth paper about the zine and its contents. How do these publications differ from mass media?

OTHER SITES RELATED TO THIS TOPIC

The Weaver
      URL: http://www.hyperlink.com/weaver/
Wired
      URL: http://www.wired.com/
World Wide Web Multi-Media Magazine
      URL: http://www.hooked.net/users/cjoga/

GALAXY'S INDEX OF ENGLISH/LITERATURE

URL: http://galaxy.einet.net/galaxy/Arts-and-Humanities/Language-and-Literature.html

Students researching a paper for a literature or English class will find plenty of help at this site. It features more than 1,000 links to English- and literature-related material. The list of topics indexed here includes an index of sites by individual author and title; collections of online texts; literature

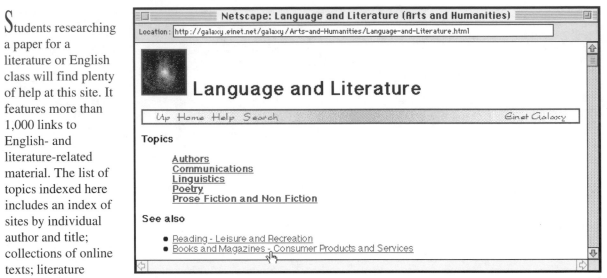

archives; periodicals of all kinds; pointers to online dictionaries and research works; and links to hundreds of English departments at universities and colleges around the world.

INTEGRATION IDEAS

● Proverbs
Have students visit the Electronic Journal of International Proverbs at this site and report upon the meaning and origin of a well-known proverb.

● Keyword search
Have students go to Literature and Journalism and do a keyword search for the same word or phrase in the Poetry and Song Lyrics databases. Have them compare how the word (e.g., love, death, money) is used in the two artistic forms.

OTHER SITES RELATED TO THIS TOPIC

World Wide Web Virtual Literature Library
URL: http://sunsite.unc.edu/ibic/IBIC-homepage.html
English/Literature Newsgroups
URL: news:rec.arts.books
URL: news:rec.arts.poems
URL: news:rec.arts.prose

GLOBAL STUDENT NEWS

URL: http://www.jou.ufl.edu/forums/gsn/

Created by journalism students at the University of Florida, the Global Student News (GNN) project brings together student journalists in high schools and colleges around the world to share ideas and content for their publications. They create a worldwide, online news desk and establish a publishing forum for students involved with reporting, editing, news photography, and more. Internet components include mailing lists or online "bureaus" for

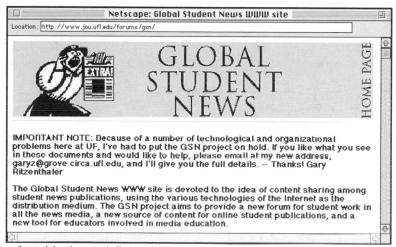

handling story traffic, a GSN newsgroup for critiquing and discussing news items, and an Internet Relay Chat channel for conducting interviews and conferences. A basic overview of GSN can be found here.

URL: http://www.jou.ufl.edu/forums/gsn/glance.htm

You can also retrieve a current list of GSN "bureaus" from the site.

URL: http://www.jou.ufl.edu/forums/gsn/director.htm

INTEGRATION IDEA

● Post work online

Have student journalists at your school sign up with the project through this Web site and submit stories to be put online. Students can use the various components of the project to improve their writing and to network with other student journalists around the world.

OTHER SITES RELATED TO THIS TOPIC

Online Resources For Student Journalists

URL: news:alt.journalism
URL: news:alt.journalism.photo
URL: news:alt.journalism.print
URL: news:alt.journalism.students
URL: http://www.jou.ufl.edu/forums/gsn/resource.htm

MYTHS AND LEGENDS

URL: http://theocean.uoregon.edu/~myth/

Created by faculty and students at the University of Oregon, the Myths and Legends Web site offers a fascinating and colorful overview of Greek and Roman myths. It's a fine and fun example of the multimedia capabilities of the Internet and is a site valuable for the sheer experience rather than for its database. But don't take students here until they've learned the basics of mythology. From its cryptic, graphical home page, to clickable maps depicting the times' notable legendary figures, the site is a great supplement to traditional instruction of junior and senior high school students studying the subject.

INTEGRATION IDEAS

• Talk to Zeus
Have students use the area of the site where they're invited to send a message to Mount Olympus. Which god or goddess would they ask a question of, and what would it be?

• Hyperlink project
After experiencing this site's extensive hyperlinks, have students design their own hyperlinked project using their own research about mythology.

OTHER SITES RELATED TO THIS TOPIC

Greek Mythology
> **URL: http://info.desy.de/gna/interpedia/greek_myth/greek_myth.html**

Myths & Legends of Indigenous Peoples
> **URL: http://www.ozemail.com.au:80/~reed/global/mythstor.html**

MythText
> **URL: http://www.the-wire.com/culture/mythology/mythtext.html**

THE POETRY CORNER

URL: http://pluto.njcc.com/~begun/welcome.html

Proud student poets can find an audience for their work via the Internet. This site features poetry written by and for Internet users. Dozens of poems are posted to the site every month, providing a creative outlet for artistic Internauts from around the world. As the authors of the site point out, their goal is simple: "We are looking to provide a database of contributed poetry. The writings we receive will be displayed on or around this page for all to enjoy. Please submit today!"

```
┌─────────────────────────────────────────────────────────────┐
│        Netscape: The Poetry Corner                            │
│ Location: http://pluto.njcc.com/~begun/welcome.html#browse    │
│                                                               │
│             the poetry corner                                 │
│                                                               │
│  Either use the menu buttons below, of scroll to get around!  │
│  Please submit your poetry!                                   │
│                                                               │
│   • Objective          Updated 4/9/95                         │
│   • Submit             Updated 4/9/95                          │
│   • Attention Users That Here On The New Poetry Notice List:   │
│     Read The News                                             │
│   • TPC News           Updated 4/14/95                        │
│   • go to the poems!   Updated 4/14/95                        │
└─────────────────────────────────────────────────────────────┘
```

INTEGRATION IDEAS

• Ask a poet
Have students read poems on the site and email an author with thoughtful questions about his or her work. What inspires the poet to write?

• Post poems
After students browse the site, have them write two poems for submission to the site. Collect their work and submit the poems to the following address.
Email to: 76325.1714@compuserve.com

OTHER SITES RELATED TO THIS TOPIC

Electronic Poetry Center
> **URL: gopher://wings.buffalo.edu/hh/internet/library/e-journals/ub/rift**

Internet Poetry Archive
> **URL: http://sunsite.unc.edu/dykki/poetry/**

William Butler Yeats
> **URL: http://www.maths.tcd.ie/pub/yeats/**

PROJECT GUTENBERG

URL: http://jg.cso.uiuc.edu/PG/welcome.html

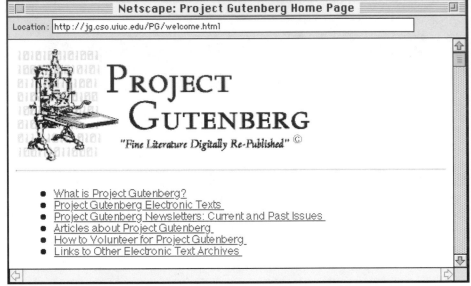

Think of this Project Gutenberg Web site as your after-hours library, open 24 hours a day, with no library card or late fees! Project Gutenberg has been bringing Free Electronic Texts (called Etexts) online since 1971 when, according to its founders, there "were only about 100 people on the Internet, and we were hoping for more!" Project Gutenberg has more than 350 books online that can be read, printed out, or downloaded for free. The works represented range from *Aesop's Fables* to the *Wonderful Wizard of Oz* by L. Frank Baum.

INTEGRATION IDEA

• Online vs. print

If the site offers books your class will be reading this year, require your students to go to Project Gutenberg and read at least two chapters of the book online. Have them write a small report comparing the differences between reading a book online and in the traditional fashion. Have them explain which they liked better, and why.

OTHER SITES RELATED TO THIS TOPIC

Censorship
    URL: http://www.cs.cmu.edu/Web/People/spok/banned-books.html
Edgar Allen Poe Home Page
    URL: http://infoweb.magi.com/~forrest/index.html
Social Sciences (Human Languages)
    URL: http://www.willamette.edu/~tjones/Language-Page.html

PURDUE ON-LINE WRITING LABORATORY

URL: http://owl.trc.purdue.edu/

The writing doctor is always in on the Internet. Student writers stumped by a grammar or spelling question can visit Purdue University's online writing lab. Here they can access research aides (from recent bills introduced in Congress to information on world health issues), Internet search tools, online writing help and other writing labs, even English as a Second Language guides and exercises. Perhaps the

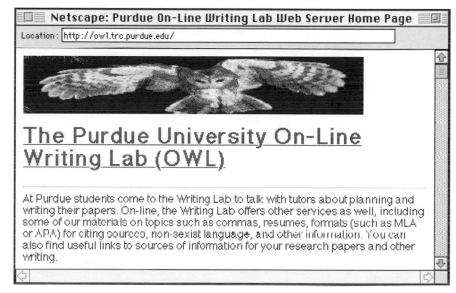

most useful part of the lab is a large (30-plus item) repository of self-help documents for student writers.
URL: http://owl.trc.purdue.edu/by-topic-alternate.html

INTEGRATION IDEAS

• ESL exercises
Have your English as a Second Language students visit the ESL section of the site. They can click on Exercises to find worksheets they can use to improve their English skills.

• Spelling practice
Have students who need spelling help go to the site's Spelling Center and click on Exercises for practice sheets.

OTHER SITES RELATED TO THIS TOPIC

Dakota State Online Writing Lab
    URL: http://www.dsu.edu:80/departments/liberal/cola/OWL/
University of Texas Undergraduate Writing Center
    URL: http://www.utexas.edu/depts/uwc/.html/main.html
The Writing Center—Online Handouts
    URL: http://www.rpi.edu/dept/11c/writecenter/web/handouts.html

TEACHING THE AMERICAN LITERATURES ARCHIVE

URL: http://www.georgetown.edu:80/tamlit/tamlit-home.html

Teachers and advanced English students will get the most value from this archive of essays, syllabi, bibliographies, and online resources for teaching the multiple literatures of the United States. There's even more than 50 online electronic texts and lesson plans for teachers of American literature.
Here's a sampling of some of the site's teaching resources: essays on teaching Asian American, Native American, and

Chicano literature; white papers on pedagogy and politics, pedagogy and relevance, and pedagogy and "national" literature; and links to dozens of online sites holding resources for American literature educators.

INTEGRATION IDEAS

• Lesson plans
Education majors who plan to teach American literature can be directed to use this site to find lesson plans for classroom use.

• Multicultural
Teachers with a special interest in multicultural instruction can use this site to find instructional ideas.

OTHER SITES RELATED TO THIS TOPIC

American Literature Survey Site
URL: http://www.en.utexas.edu/~daniel/amlit/amlit.html
American Literature Annotated by High School Students
URL: http://www.en.utexas.edu/~daniel/amlit/stories.html
Online Library for Teaching the American Literatures
URL: http://www.georgetown.edu/tamlit/teaching/syllabi_lib.html

C H A P T E R

FOREIGN LANGUAGES

- Arabic Audio Lessons
- Echo Eurodictautom
- English-Spanish Dictionary
- *English as a Foreign Language Magazine*
- French-English Dictionary
- French Language Web

- German-English Dictionary
- Hindi Lessons
- Japan Information Center
- Mexican Spanish Tutor
- The Human-Languages Page
- Universal Survey of Languages

A R A B I C   A U D I O   L E S S O N S

URL: http://philae.sas.upenn.edu/Arabic/arabic.html

Whether students are simply curious about Arabic or are advanced students of the language, this site appeals to anyone who wants to learn about Arabic. It includes a six-tiered, audio class that can be completed online, as well as advanced multimedia files with music and film clips. The site includes photographs of architecture, paintings, rugs, and other cultural artifacts that aid in understanding the Arab world.

```
┌──────────────────────────────────────────────────────┐
│ ▤▤▤▤▤▤▤▤▤▤ Netscape: arabic.html ▤▤▤▤▤▤▤▤▤▤ │
├──────────────────────────────────────────────────────┤
│ Location : │http://philae.sas.upenn.edu/Arabic/arabic.html│ │
├──────────────────────────────────────────────────────┤
│ Arabic Program at Penn                                 │
│                                                        │
│ ────────────────────────────────────────────────────  │
│ Copyright: R. Allen, 1994                              │
│                                                        │
│    ● About Roger Allen                                 │
│    ● About the Arabic Program                          │
│    ● About courses and majoring in Arabic              │
│                                                        │
│ Let's Learn Arabic (Hypertext version)                 │
│                                                        │
│        لتتعلّم العربية                                  │
│                                                        │
│ ────────────────────────────────────────────────────  │
│ Arabic Audio Lessons                                   │
│                                                        │
│ Arabic Music, Films & Pictures                         │
└──────────────────────────────────────────────────────┘
```

INTEGRATION IDEAS

● World cultures
Have students visit the site and go through the audio course, pronouncing basic words and phrases. What languages are similar? How does Arabic compare to other language families, such as Romance?

● Teacher aids
Online software (DOS) to aid in the teaching of Arabic is available at the following site.
URL: gopher://ccat.sas.upenn.edu
An Arabic Tutor is also available.
URL: http://darkwing.uoregon.edu/~alquds/ arabic.html

OTHER SITES RELATED TO THIS TOPIC

Art (Arab Music Files)
  URL: http://philae.sas.upenn.edu/Arabic/arabfilm.html
Arabic Web Link Index
  URL: http://darkwing.uoregon.edu/~alquds/
Palestinian Web Sites
  URL: http://http1.brunel.ac.uk:8080/~em93mma

ECHO EURODICTAUTOM

URL: http://www.uni-frankfurt.de/~felix/eurodictautom.html

More than eight languages are at students' fingertips via this site's interactive database. It allows users to translate words from one language to another in real time. Think of it as a universal translator that can convert almost any word into English, French, German, Italian, Spanish, Danish, and Portuguese. A telnet version of the site is also available. It offers even more flexibility in translation, though it is harder to use.
URL: telnet://echo.lu

```
┌──────────────────────────────────────────────────────┐
│       Netscape: ECHO - EURODICAUTOM                   │
├──────────────────────────────────────────────────────┤
│ Location: http://www.uni-frankfurt.de/~felix/eurodictautom.html │
├──────────────────────────────────────────────────────┤
│ Check here for activating abbreviations mode ☐        │
│                                                        │
│ Try the new (also experimental) Gateway. And please mail us your │
│ comments!                                              │
│ Please enter query : [Computer        ]  (Please translate │
│ umlauts and other special characters by yourself as told in the │
│ special char translation table)                       │
│                                                        │
│ Select a Source and a Target language (not available in abbreviations mode) │
│                                                        │
│ Source Language     Target Language                   │
│ ┌─────────────┐     ┌─────────────┐                   │
│ │ English    ⇧│     │ English    ⇧│                   │
│ │ French      │     │ French      │                   │
│ │ German      │     │ German      │                   │
│ │ Italian     │     │ Italian     │                   │
│ │ Spanish     │     │ Spanish     │                   │
│ │ Danish      │     │ Danish      │                   │
│ │ Dutch       │     │ Dutch       │                   │
│ │ Portuguese ⇩│     │ Portuguese ⇩│                   │
│ └─────────────┘     └─────────────┘                   │
│                                                        │
│ ( start query )                                        │
│ ( reset form )                                         │
└──────────────────────────────────────────────────────┘
```

INTEGRATION IDEAS

● Translation

Have students use the site to translate 10-15 words into at least four languages. Have them mix them up and try to match them with the correct language.

● Keypals

Find keypals in a country whose natives speak one of the languages at this site. Have classes exchange email in their native tongues, using the site to translate messages.

OTHER SITES RELATED TO THIS TOPIC

Experimental Enhanced Echo Eurodictautom Interface
URL: http://www.uni-frankfurt.de/~kurlanda/eurodicautom.html
Portuguese Eurodictautom
URL: http://www.public.iastate.edu/~pedro/pt_all/pt_dict.html

ENGLISH-SPANISH DICTIONARY

URL: http://www.willamette.edu/~tjones/forms/spanish.html

This small yet expanding English-to-Spanish Dictionary will help any student with Spanish courses. Type a word or part of a word in the text box, choose whether to search for that word exactly or to search for words containing that part of a word, and select the "Search" button to search the dictionary. (Note that searches are case-insensitive.)

> **Netscape: English-to-Spanish Dictionary**
>
> Location: http://www.willamette.edu/~tjones/forms/spanish.html
>
> This is a very small Spanish dictionary, with a very simple interface. Type a word or part of a word in the text area below, choose whether to search for that word exactly or to search for words containing that part of a word, and select the "Search" button to search the dictionary. The difference between "search by whole word" and not searching by whole word is: "search by whole word" with a keyword of "and" returns only "and". Without searching by whole word, the search will return "and", "hand", "husband", etc. This dictionary contains approximately 1300 terms. Searches are case-insensitive.
>
> This dictionary is experimental. I know that it doesn't always work correctly, so I'm trying to figure out why. How can you help? By reporting any crashes, error messages, hangs, or other problems to me, tjones@willamette.edu. Thanks.
>
> Enter English word to search for: Food
>
> Search for whole word only? Yes ● No ○
>
> [Search]
>
> Spanish-to-English Dictionary

INTEGRATION IDEA

• Word search
Divide the class into two groups and give them a vocabulary list of new Spanish words. One group uses a traditional dictionary and the other this site. Which has more accurate answers? Which was more efficient? Have the groups create new word lists and switch dictionaries.

OTHER SITES RELATED TO THIS TOPIC

Pedro's Online Language Dictionaries
  URL: http://www.public.iastate.edu/~pedro/dictionaries.html
Spain & Spanish on the Internet Index
  URL: http://gias720.dis.ulpgc.es/spain.html
Tecla Spanish Educator/Student Magazine
  URL: http://www.bbk.ac.uk/Departments/Spanish/TeclaHome.html

ENGLISH AS A FOREIGN LANGUAGE MAGAZINE

URL: http://www.u-net.com/eflweb/

Educators and students will find great value in this resource about teaching and learning English as a foreign language. You'll find straightforward answers to commonly asked questions, such as: "Where do I go to learn English? What online resources are available on this topic? What are some hands-on experiences of teachers and students? Where can I go to take courses to teach/learn English as a foreign language?"

INTEGRATION IDEA

• Keypals

Have native English speakers use this site to delve into learning English as a foreign language. Then, have the students send email to students of English abroad to learn what it takes to learn the language. What do they find most difficult? Have students help them with their questions about English.

OTHER SITES RELATED TO THIS TOPIC

Directory of Schools Teaching English as a Foreign Language Courses
> **URL: http://www.u-net.com/eflweb/tefl20.htm**

Foreign Language Teaching Forum
> **URL: http://www.cortland.edu/www_root/flteach/flteach.html**

Teaching English in Japan
> **URL: http://www.u-net.com/eflweb/japan0.htm**

FRENCH-ENGLISH DICTIONARY

URL: http://tuna.uchicago.edu/forms_unrest/FR-ENG.html

This robust French to English dictionary will help any student with his or her French courses. It features more than 75,000 words. Type a word or part of a word with an * on the end in the text box, and select the "Submit Query" button to search. (Note that searches are case-insensitive.)

```
┌──────────────────────────────────────────────────────────────────┐
│ ☐        Netscape: ARTFL Project: French-English Dictionary Form  │
│ Location: │http://tuna.uchicago.edu/forms_unrest/FR-ENG.html│     │
│                                                                    │
│ ARTFL Project: French-English Dictionary                           │
│ Form                                                               │
│                                                                    │
│ Look up words in a simple French English Dictionary containing about 75,000 terms. │
│                                                                    │
│ Search for: │oui                        │ (ex. amour or raison*)  │
│                                                                    │
│ The asterix (*) matches all suffixes and may only appear at the end of your search term. │
│                                                                    │
│ To submit the query, press [ Submit Query ]                        │
└──────────────────────────────────────────────────────────────────┘
```

INTEGRATION IDEA

• **Short story**
Have students write a short story in French and check each other's work using this site. Was the site missing any of the words? If so, submit them to Tyler Jones, author of the site.

OTHER SITES RELATED TO THIS TOPIC

American Association of Teachers of French
    URL: gopher://utsainfo.utsa.edu:7070/1/
French Soccer Web Server
    URL: http://www.cc.columbia.edu/~yn25/soccer.html
Hapax: French Resources on the Web
    URL: http://hapax.be.sbc.edu/home.html

FRENCH LANGUAGE WEB

URL: http://web.cnam.fr/fr/

A link to all things French, this Web site is maintained by a major university in France and is written completely in the native language. It features pointers to practical information about traveling the country, hyperlinks to popular tourist attractions, online language lessons and links to French language tutoring software, and much more. The site includes links to many hands-on French language lessons for students.
URL:
http://insti.physics.sunysb.edu/
~mmartin/languages/languages.html
URL:
http://www2.montefiore.ulg.ac.be/
~bronne/francais.html

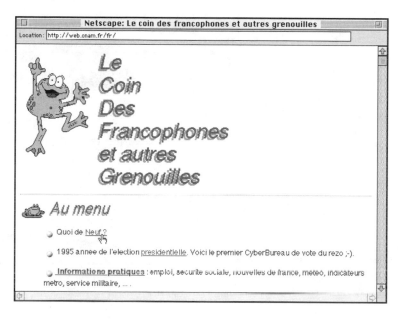

INTEGRATION IDEAS

• French cooking
Have students go to Les Arts de la Table and then Cuisine. Have them translate the recipes, convert the metric measurements, cook the dish, and create a cookbook of French recipes.

• Current events
Have students access the latest French news stories and translate enough to be able to tell and discuss what they mean.
URL: http://world-net.sct.fr/elysee/
URL: http://www.b3e.jussieu.fr:80/
cgi-bin/je_vote

OTHER SITES RELATED TO THIS TOPIC

Art (French Art)
URL: http://web.cnam.fr/fr/frarts.html
Social Sciences/Humanities (French Politics)
URL: http://solcidsp.grenet.fr:8001
French Language Reader (Mac)
URL: ftp://ftp.wentworth.com/wentworth/Internet-Software/Mac/FrenchReader.hqx

GERMAN-ENGLISH DICTIONARY

URL: http://calamity.rz-berlin.mpg.de/eg.html

Direct from Germany, this German to English (and English to German) dictionary is a handy tool for students of German. Like the online French dictionary, you type a word or part of a word in the text box, choose whether you want the search to be case sensitive or for an exact match, then select the "Submit Query" button to search the dictionary's more than 100,000 terms.

```
Netscape: Dictionary
Location: http://calamity.rz-berlin.mpg.de/eg.html

                      Dictionary

     This is a simple english-german, german-english dictionary

Name: Automobile

   [ Case Insensitve  ▼ ]  [ ✓ Search Substring ▼ ]  [ Submit Query ]
                              Search Exact
```

INTEGRATION IDEA

● Word stretch
Have students write a short story using at least ten German words they have never used. Have them trade papers and translate the stories using this site. Then make flash cards of the new words and have a quiz bowl.

OTHER SITES RELATED TO THIS TOPIC

Knowledge Network Library
    URL: http://www.kn.pacbell.com/library.html
Germany Home Page
    URL: http://www.chemie.fu-berlin.de/adressen/brd.html
Online Dictionary Pointers
    URL: http://www.lib.occ.cccd.edu/Library/Dict.html

HINDI LESSONS

URL: http://philae.sas.upenn.edu/Hindi/hindi.html

Although designed for undergraduate university students, any high school student interested in learning more about the Hindi language will find value at this site. Included are more than three dozen online Hindi lessons (many include sound bites!) and several video lessons that students can download and view. Several "photo albums" of northern India are worth viewing. The photo album index features hyperlinked captions that take you directly to the photos.

Netscape: Hindi Program at Penn

Location: http://philae.sas.upenn.edu/Hindi/hindi.html

Hindi Program at Penn

Copyright: S. Gambhir, 1994

- About Surendra Gambhir
- About the Hindi Program at Penn
- Nagari script

Audio Lessons

- Informal construction
- Constants like 'ke','kar'
- Time expressions
- Present participles
- Hypothetical sentences
- Compound postpositions
- Roger Karen Lesson 1.1
- Roger Karen Lesson 1.2

INTEGRATION IDEAS

• Tutorial

Have your students complete one to three of the most basic Hindi lessons here. How different from English is Hindi? How similar?

• Travelogue

Have students survey the photos at this site. How does the architecture and art of India differ from others? What impact does religion have on art?

OTHER SITES RELATED TO THIS TOPIC

Hindi Films & Music
　　　URL: http://www.cs.cornell.edu/Info/People/verma/music.html#audio
Hindi Fonts
　　　URL: http://babel.uoregon.edu/yamada/guides/hindiurdu.html
Links to India
　　　URL: http://www.fcaglp.unlp.edu.ar/~spaoli/indialinks.html

JAPAN INFORMATION CENTER

URL: http://fuji.stanford.edu/

Elementary students will love the Japanese language and culture activities at this beautifully designed site. Just click on the Japan window and then click on the Just for Kids icon. Your young students can learn how to read and create (and can listen to!) hiragana, katakana, and kanji. The Restaurant portion of the site shows students typical Japanese meals and teaches several terms. Students can also follow visual step-by-step instructions on how to do origami.

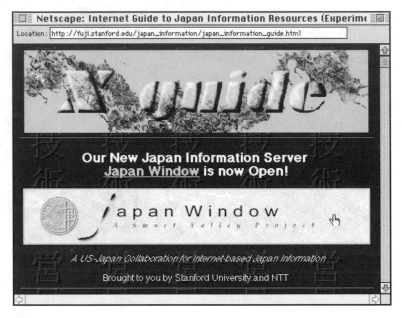

INTEGRATION IDEA

• Hiragana

Have students make a book of several hiragana. Students can take turns teaching one to the class. Compare each student's copy of the same hiragana, looking for differences. Would they look the same to a Japanese person, or would the person see them as different characters? How does this make Japanese difficult to learn?

OTHER SITES RELATED TO THIS TOPIC

Japanese-English Dictionary
        URL: http://www.wg.omron.co.jp/cgi-bin/j-e/tty/dict
Kobe, Japan Earthquake
        URL: http://www-leland.stanford.edu/~shimpei/quake.html
Traveler's Japanese Online Course
        URL: http://www.ntt.jp/japan/japanese/

MEXICAN SPANISH TUTOR

URL: http://www.willamette.edu/~tjoncs/Spanish/Spanish-main.html

Written by a college professor for high school students studying Spanish, the Mexican Spanish Tutor is your link to three hands-on language lessons. Each lesson includes new words and simple phrases, along with definitions, pronunciation tips, and online audio clips of what the words should sound like. As the project continues, more advanced items will be added, including verbs and sentence structures. Be aware that some Spanish language characters will not show up correctly when viewed with a text-based Web browser such as Lynx. For best results, use a graphical Internet account running Netscape or Mosaic browser software to visit this site.

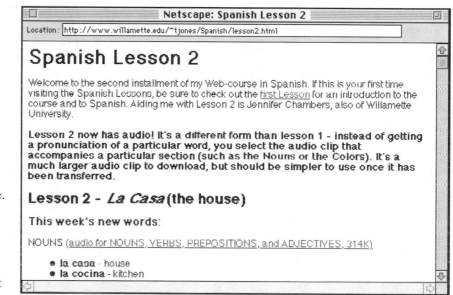

Netscape: Spanish Lesson 2
Location: http://www.willamette.edu/~tjones/Spanish/lesson2.html

Spanish Lesson 2

Welcome to the second installment of my Web-course in Spanish. If this is your first time visiting the Spanish Lessons, be sure to check out the first Lesson for an introduction to the course and to Spanish. Aiding me with Lesson 2 is Jennifer Chambers, also of Willamette University.

Lesson 2 now has audio! It's a different form than lesson 1 - instead of getting a pronunciation of a particular word, you select the audio clip that accompanies a particular section (such as the Nouns or the Colors). It's a much larger audio clip to download, but should be simpler to use once it has been transferred.

Lesson 2 - *La Casa* (the house)

This week's new words:

NOUNS (audio for NOUNS, VERBS, PREPOSITIONS, and ADJECTIVES, 314K)

- **la casa** - house
- **la cocina** - kitchen

INTEGRATION IDEAS

● Vocabulary exercise

Have students study the vocabulary list and grammar section at this site. At the end of the lesson, students can take a test online and check each other's answers.

● Make a test

Have students create their own test using information from the site and then exchange with another student.

OTHER SITE RELATED TO THIS TOPIC

Italian Language Lessons
URL: http://www.willamette.edu/~tjones/languages/Italian/Italian-lesson.html

THE HUMAN-LANGUAGES PAGE

URL: http://www.willamette.edu/~tjones/Language-Page.html

Revisit the Tower of Babel via this Web site. It has links to more than 200 Internet repositories of information about 60 world languages. You'll find dozens of language dictionaries, lessons, links to native literature and poetry, and software for Mac and Windows to help students learn the basics of each language, including Afrikaans, Arabic, Bulgarian, Catalan, Chinese, Croatian, Danish, Dutch, English, Esperanto, Estonian, French, Gaelic, German, Greek, Hawaiian, Hebrew, Hindi, Indonesian, Italian, Japanese, Kurdish, Latin, Lojban, Maori, Mongolian, Native American languages, Nepali, Norwegian, Persian, Philippine, Polish, Portuguese, Rasta/Patois, Romanian, Russian, Sardinian, Scandinavian, Serbian, Slovak, Slovene, Spanish, Swahili, Swedish, Tagalog, Tamil, Tibetan, Turkish, Urdu, Viennese, Vietnamese, and Welsh. Whew! The site includes links to many hands-on language lessons for students.

Integral Dutch Course
URL: http://unicks.calvin.edu/dutchcourse.html
A Little Bit of Hebrew
URL: http://www.macom.co.il/hebrew/
Serbian Language Tutor
URL: http://www.umiacs.umd.edu/research/lpv/YU/HTML/jezik.html

INTEGRATION IDEAS

● Compare and contrast
Have students pick a language listed on the site for further study. Have them write a paper detailing the similarities and differences between the language they're studying and English.

● Esperanto
Have students visit the Esperanto area and take the Hypercourse to learn definitions and simple words. They can even try posting comments in the language.

OTHER SITES RELATED TO THIS TOPIC

English/Literature (English Vocabulary)
URL: http://www.wordsmith.org
Geography (Middle East Resource Center)
URL: http://gpg.com/MERC/

UNIVERSAL SURVEY OF LANGUAGES

URL: http://www.teleport.com/~napoleon/

The goal of this developing project is to create a general survey of the world's languages suitable for the linguistic beginner and the expert. It's a worthwhile stop for students interested in more obscure languages, such as those of Native Americans and of the Basques. Included at the site are academic papers about the languages, new developments in languages, audio clips, and miscellaneous material. The site includes links to several hands-on language lessons for students.
URL: http://www.teleport.com/~napoleon/ natlang.html

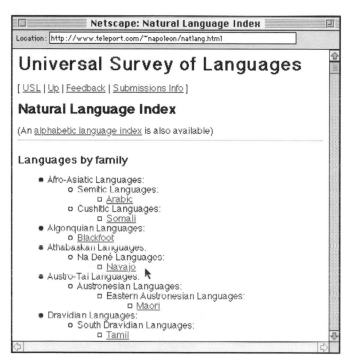

INTEGRATION IDEA

● **Ethnic culture**
Have students use this site to research the Basque, Creole, Catalan, Blackfoot, and Navajo languages. How do these ethnic groups keep their languages alive? Is government support, such as that of French in Canada, effective? Have students research bills proposing English as a national or state language.

OTHER SITES RELATED TO THIS TOPIC

Language Resource Center Online
   URL: http://grafton.dartmouth.edu:8001/lrc
Modern Languages Resources
   URL: http://labdir.modlang.swt.edu/default.html
Natural Language Processing Home Page
   URL: http://www-cac.sci.kun.nl/cac/www-nl-cl.html

C H A P T E R

GEOGRAPHY

- Antarctica Maps
- CityLink Project
- City.Net
- Color Relief Map of the United States
- ElNet Galaxy Index to
  World Communities
- GNN Travel Center Home Page
- KidsCom
- National Mapping Information
- Project GeoSim
- U.S. Census Bureau Home Page

ANTARCTICA MAPS

URL: http://www.hmc.edu/www/people/teverett/antarctica/Maps.html

To really go down under, visit this site and view more than a dozen online maps of Antarctica. The perspectives of the maps vary, from views from in orbit to on the ground. Many of the maps were

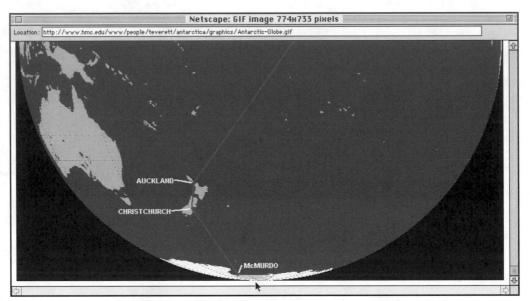

scanned in and put online by members of the Ross Island team, which has made the continent its home.

INTEGRATION IDEAS

● Change
Divide the continent into quarters and assign students a portion to research and view over time. Does the continent's size change throughout the year?

● Distance
Have students use the maps to measure the continent's relative distances from nearby continents.

OTHER SITES RELATED TO THIS TOPIC

Antarctica Resource Guide
    URL: http://http2.sils.umich.edu/Antarctica/Bibliography/Bib.html
Gateway to Antarctica
    URL: http://icair.iac.org.nz/
New South Polar Times
    URL: http://www.deakin.edu.au/edu/MSEE/GENII/NSPT/NSPThomePage.html

C I T Y L I N K P R O J E C T

URL: http://www.neosoft.com:80/citylink/

For a comprehensive online tour of cities in all 50 states and the U.S. Virgin Islands, check out the USA CityLink Project. Click on the state of your choice to find links to dozens of cities in that state. You'll find pictures of famous landmarks, online local newspapers, demographic information, and links to city and state government organizations.

INTEGRATION IDEAS

• Your city online

Have students create a Web guide to their city and submit it to the USA CityLink Project for mounting online. They can use the site's press release template to inform local media of their online successes.

• Compare and contrast

Let students explore numerous cities and pick one they would like to live in. Have them compare it to your city's history, economy, geography, lifestyle, and weather. Why would they like to visit or live there?

OTHER SITES RELATED TO THIS TOPIC

EINet Galaxy's Guide to U.S. States
URL: http://galaxy.einet.net/galaxy/Community/US-States/
Geography Resources at the Library of Congress
URL: gopher://marvel.loc.gov:70/11/global/geohist
Geographic Name Server
URL: telnet://martini.eecs.umich.edu:3000

CITY.NET

URL: http://www.city.net

This guide to cities, countries, and communities around the world is fast becoming one of the most popular sites on the Web. Students will love exploring the geography and culture of other towns, cities, and nations—from Aachen, Germany, to Zvolen, Slovakia. Thousands of links are included. Students can find information by browsing an alphabetical index, selecting an area on a clickable world map, or using City.Net's keyword search feature. One unrelated but very handy link lets you check for the latest versions of popular Web browsers, and even tests your browser to see if you're up-to-date.

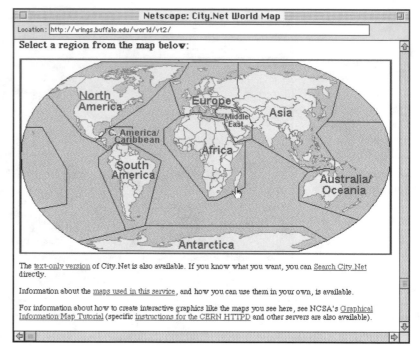

INTEGRATION IDEAS

• Travel agents
Have students pick a country or region and use the site to create travel brochures and presentations for imaginary clients and the class.

• Genealogy
Have students use the site to explore their families' nation of origin and look for interesting facts or tidbits about their heritage.

OTHER SITES RELATED TO THIS TOPIC

CIA World Factbook
URL: http://www.ic.gov:80/94fact/fb94toc/fb94toc.html
State Department Travel Advisories
URL: gopher://gopher.stolaf.edu/11/Internet Resources/US-State-Department-Travel-Advisories
Starting Points for Geographic Information Systems & Cartography
URL: http://www.iko.unit.no/gis/gisen.html

COLOR RELIEF MAP OF THE UNITED STATES

URL: http://www.zilker.net/~hal/apl-us/

Younger students will love clicking on this color relief map of the U.S. and zooming into different regions and getting a better look at mountains and valleys recently mapped by NASA. Truly an interactive, fun way to manipulate an online map.

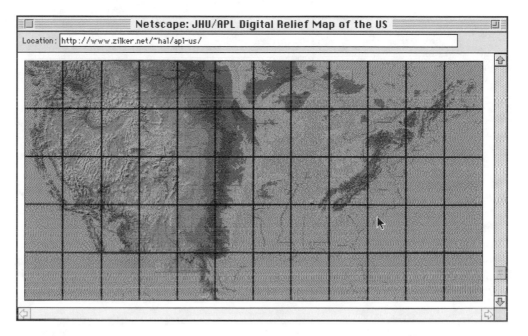

INTEGRATION IDEA

• **Take a tour**

During your normal course of study about maps, have your students access this site and manipulate this map, both as an interesting interface to relief map data, and as a great example of an advanced Web site.

OTHER SITES RELATED TO THIS TOPIC

Canada Maps
> **URL: http://ellesmere.ccm.emr.ca/wwwnais/wwwnais.html**

Mapmaker, Mapmaker, Make Me a Map
> **URL: http://loki.ur.utk.edu/ut2kids/maps/map.html**

Map-Related Web Sites
> **URL: http://rowan.lib.utexas.edu/Libs/PCL/MAP_collection/map_sites.html**

EINET GALAXY INDEX TO WORLD COMMUNITIES

URL: http://galaxy.einet.net/galaxy/Community/World-Communities.html

EINet Galaxy certainly offers plenty of valuable indexes for locating resources online, but its guide to world communities is one of the best. Students and teachers could spend endless hours learning about faraway places. Besides geography, these hyperlinks will take you to information on topics such as language, culture, world economics and trade, environmental issues, and geology. You'll find lots of photos, graphics, flags, and maps—and even some links to schools from around the world.

```
Netscape: World Communities (Community)
Location: http://galaxy.einet.net/galaxy/Community/World-Communities.html

World Communities

Up  Home  Help  Search                                    Einet Ga

Topics
   Africa
          Ethiopia - Rwanda - Somalia - South Africa
   Asia
          Armenia - Bangladesh - India - Malaysia - Nepal - Pakistan - Philippines - Thailand - Tibet -
          Vietnam
   Central America
          Costa Rica - Guatemala - Mexico
   Europe
          Austria - Belgium - Bulgaria - Croatia - Cyprus - Czech Republic - Denmark - Finland -
          France - Germany - Greece - Hungary - Iceland - Ireland - Italy - Lithuania - Monaco -
          Norway - Poland - Portugal - Russia - Slovakia - Spain - Sweden - Switzerland - The
          Netherlands - Turkey - United Kingdom - Yugoslavia
   Middle East
          Egypt - Israel - Kuwait - Lebanon
```

INTEGRATION IDEAS

• Foreign keypals
Find keypals in a country your students are studying. Have students use this site to learn about their pals' home nation and submit questions to them.

• Current events
Have students search this site for information about nations in crisis, e.g., Rwanda, Yugoslavia. Do the sites reflect the crises in those countries? Why or why not?

OTHER SITES RELATED TO THIS TOPIC

University at Buffalo Geography Resources on the Internet
   URL: http://www.geog.buffalo.edu
World Wide Web Virtual Library: Geography
   URL: http://hpb1.hwc.ca:10002/WWW_VL_Geography.html

GNN TRAVEL CENTER HOME PAGE

URL: http://nearnet.gnn.com/gnn/meta/travel/index.html

Geographical material abounds at the links at the GNN Travel Center site. For starters, try Fodor's Worldbook, which publishes up-to-date information on travel destinations worldwide. Select Latin America, for example, to get a list of dozens of destinations in

Mexico, Central America, and South America. Click on Acapulco and you'll learn that brave souls dive every day from the high cliffs surrounding Acapulco's bays—even the sky-high cliff where the Virgin of Guadalupe looks out over the water.

INTEGRATION IDEAS

• Travel planning
Use this site and other travel sites to have students pick a destination and make a travel plan. They should research weather, hotel costs, exchange rates, etc.

• Travel writing
The Notes from the Road section features articles and photo essays reflecting a specific area. Does the material give readers a feeling for the geography of region? Have students write an intimate travel piece about where they live.

OTHER SITES RELATED TO THIS TOPIC

Adventurous Traveler Map List
URL: http://www.gorp.com/atb/maps.htm
Mountain Travel Sobek
URL: http://www.mtsobek.com/mts/
PCL Map Collection
URL: http://www.lib.utexas.edu/Libs/PCL/Map_collection.html

KIDSCOM

URL: http://www.kidscom.com

Looking for a fun way to teach younger students (grades 2-6) about geography? KidsCom is home to an interactive geography game which challenges kids to guess the name of the capital city of more than three dozen countries. It even keeps score as they play! This site is wonderful tool that helps younger students become comfortable with the World Wide Web. KidsCom's Ask Tobie Wan Kenobi page even

gives kids a way to ask a young Internet expert where to find things on the Internet.

INTEGRATION IDEAS

• Geography game
Have each student play the game and put their knowledge up against the thousands of kids who put their names on the high score list.

• Geography search
Assign students the task of answering a geography question via an Internet search. They can ask Tobie Wan for help.

OTHER SITES RELATED TO THIS TOPIC

Geography Sites
> **URL: gopher://gopher.stanford.edu:4320/1geo%20**
> **URL: news:bit.listserv.geograph**
> **URL: http://www.delorme.com/maps/geourls.htm**

English/Literature (Keypals)
> **URL: http://www.spectracom.com/kidscom/keypal.html**

NATIONAL MAPPING INFORMATION

URL: http://www-nmd.usgs.gov

The U.S. Geological Survey offers a multitude of educational materials to aid in the teaching of geography to young students. It publishes informative teaching packets, posters, booklets, leaflets, and brochures about many aspects of the earth sciences. The publications are designed to be of

interest to teachers, students, and the public and may be obtained free from any Earth Science Information Center (ESIC). For more information call 1-800-USA-MAPS, or visit this Web site and retrieve it all!

INTEGRATION IDEA

• Teaching materials
Some examples of the site's resources, with emphasis on mapping, geography, and global change, include teaching packets on What Maps Show, Global Change, and Exploring Maps, and booklets on Helping Your Child Learn Geography, Topographic Mapping, and Elevations and Distances in the United States.
URL: http://www-nmd.usgs.gov/www/html/leducate.html

OTHER SITES RELATED TO THIS TOPIC

National Mapping Program Activities
      URL: http://www-nmd.usgs.gov/www/html/nmp_prog.html
U.S. Geological Information Home Page
      URL: http://geology.usgs.gov
U.S. Geological Survey Home Page
      URL: http://www.usgs.gov

PROJECT GEOSIM

URL: http://geosim.cs.vt.edu

What would happen if Montana became the most populous state in the country? It would wield more political power in Washington. Project GeoSim allows educators to use data to teach powerful geography lessons. A joint project of the departments of

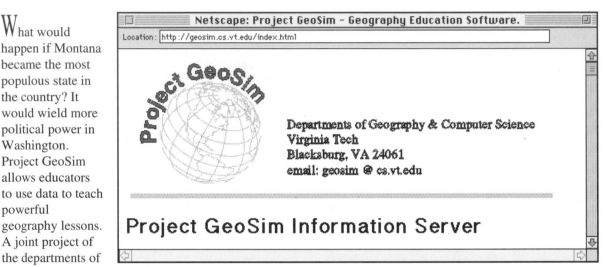

Netscape: Project GeoSim – Geography Education Software.

Location: http://geosim.cs.vt.edu/index.html

Departments of Geography & Computer Science
Virginia Tech
Blacksburg, VA 24061
email: geosim @ cs.vt.edu

Project GeoSim Information Server

computer science and geography at Virginia Tech, the site offers educators at least four simulation programs they can download and use. Mental Maps is a geography quiz game. International Population and Migration Modeling are demographics simulations. Congressional Apportionment teaches how population growth affects political power. Sense of Place employs statistics to give snapshots of counties in the United States. The software runs on MS-DOS, Macintosh, and X-Windows.

INTEGRATION IDEAS

• Mental Maps
Download Mental Maps and have students test their geography knowledge with this program.

• International Population
Download International Population. Have groups of students use different variables in fertility, birth, death, and migration rates and compare their results. How do these factors affect quality of life?
URL: http://geosim.cs.vt.edu/index.html

OTHER SITES RELATED TO THIS TOPIC

GeoSim Gopher Resources
        URL: gopher://geosim.cs.vt.edu:70/1
GeoSim Organizers Home Page
        URL: http://gopher.vt.edu/index.html
GeoSim Mailing List
        URL: mailto:geosim@cs.vt.edu

U.S. CENSUS BUREAU HOME PAGE

URL: http://www.census.gov

Future geographers and cartographers will find plenty to interest them here. Choose the Geography button on the home page to try out the Tiger Mapping Service, "a public resource for generating high-quality, detailed maps." Or try the GeoWeb, which takes you to information on the GeoWeb mailing list, which helps users locate other geographic information on the Net. The DataMaps State Profiles hyperlink, though, is by far the best. First you get a colorful U.S. map. Click on a state for an enlarged view showing counties, then select a county to get detailed census information on population, housing, education, labor force, income and poverty levels, and much more.

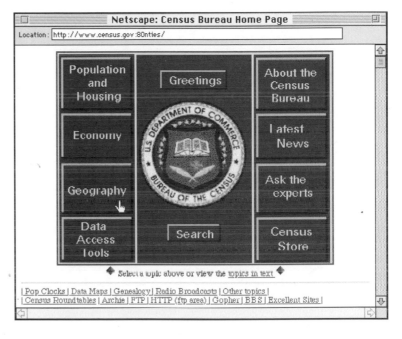

INTEGRATION IDEAS

● Rich and poor

Have students pick a state and research its counties to find the most and the least affluent based on factors such as income, education, etc. What problems are faced by each?

● Ask an expert

Have students visit the Ask an Expert area and email demographics questions they cannot answer via research.

OTHER SITES RELATED TO THIS TOPIC

County & City Data Book
    URL: http://www.census.gov/stat_abstract/ccdb/
Department of Geography at the University of South Carolina
    URL: http://lorax.geog.scarolina.edu/index.html

CHAPTER 6

HEALTH/PHYSICAL EDUCATION

- AIDS Education Training Project
- Audio Health Files
- *Balance*
- Children's Medical Center
- Global Health Network
- Health Explorer
- HealthLinks

- International Food Information Council
- OncoLink Cancer Resource Center
- Substance Abuse Prevention Center
- TraumaNet
- U.S. Health Statistics
- Virtual Hospital
- Women's Health Hot Line Home Page

AIDS EDUCATION TRAINING PROJECT

URL: http://www.ach.uams.edu/~bnd/aids

AIDS is the foremost public health problem facing the United States, according to the Department of Health and Human Services. No longer confined to a specific population or group, AIDS and HIV infection are spreading rapidly to all facets of society. This Web site has been set up to disseminate basic (what it is, how people contract it) and advanced (microscopic views of the virus) information about AIDS. This site is a must visit for all students learning about this deadly virus.

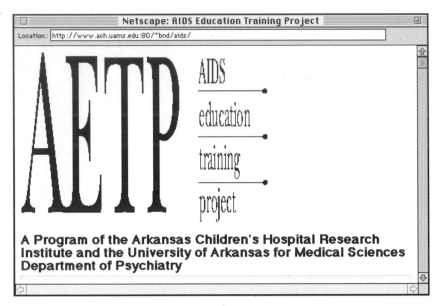

INTEGRATION IDEAS

• Transmission

Have students use this site to find and list adolescent behavior that makes young people "at risk" for HIV and AIDS. How would they help a friend they knew was putting him or herself at risk?

• Scrapbook

Have students use this site and other media to compile a report on how AIDS affects infants, children, young people, and families.

OTHER SITES RELATED TO THIS TOPIC

AIDS Information Newsletter
    URL: http://cornelius.ucsf.edu/~troyer/safesex/vanews/
Index of Online AIDS Resources
    URL: http://www.cmpharm.ucsf.edu/~troyer/safesex/otherresources.html
Women & AIDS Studies
    URL: http://www.cmpharm.ucsf.edu/~troyer/safesex/vanews/vanewswomen.html

AUDIO HEALTH FILES

URL: http://www.tcom.ohiou.edu/family-health.html

Students can use this site to listen to health information—an ideal opportunity for students with impaired vision to access the World Wide Web. Family Health is a daily, online series of 2 1/2-minute audio programs featuring practical, easy-to-understand answers to some of the most frequently asked questions about health and health care. While rarer diseases are occasionally covered, the series focuses on the common health problems people are likely to ask of family physicians. Currently, the audio files are available in **.au** (Macintosh) format only. Examples of available recordings include: Chicken Wings, Cleaning Your Ears, Electromagnetic Fields, Moderate Alcohol Intake, Multiple Sclerosis, Pesticide Residues, Restless Leg Syndrome, and Sprained Ankles. Be sure to check the index for a full listing of available programs.

URL: http://www.tcom.ohiou.edu/family-health/fh-index.html

INTEGRATION IDEAS

• Poster project
Have students listen to programs on topics such as bicycle helmets, handwashing, and Halloween safety. Have them pick a topic and make a poster promoting health and safety for the class or school.

• Public service announcement
Have students research a health or safety issue and create their own 2 1/2-minute audio program on the topic.

OTHER SITES RELATED TO THIS TOPIC

Attention Deficit Disorder Archive
URL: http://www.seas.upenn.edu/~mengwong/add/
Computers & Health
URL: http://www-penninfo.upenn.edu:1962/tiserve.mit.edu/9000/25204.html
Consumer Health Information
URL: gopher://gopher.health.state.ny.us

BALANCE

URL: http://tito.hyperlink.com/balance/

This online magazine covers all aspects of health and fitness, including exercise and injury prevention, diet and nutrition, stress reduction, and disease prevention. Challenge students to take the *Balance* Fitness and Health Quiz to see how much they really know about staying fit. The site is light on graphics but contains lots of full-text articles. New issues come out the first of every month.

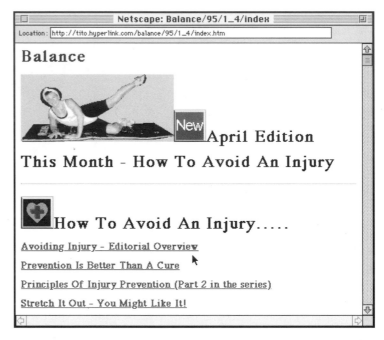

INTEGRATION IDEAS

• Student publishing
Have students create their own health and fitness quiz for the rest of their class. They can mount it on the school Web page for other Internauts to tackle.

• Prevention
After students tour this site, have them analyze their family's lifestyle and develop a plan to improve its wellness.

OTHER SITES RELATED TO THIS TOPIC

Injury & Disease Links
URL: http://www.telepath.com:80/gdj1146/pyc/
Nutrition, Diet, Food Labeling
URL: http://vm.cfsan.fda.gov/label.html
Weightlifting
URL: http://www.cs.odu.edu:80/~ksw/weights.html

CHILDREN'S MEDICAL CENTER

URL: http://galen.med.virginia.edu/~smb4v/cmchome.html

The Children's Medical Center is truly the world's first "hospital without walls." While the CMC operates as part of the University of Virginia Health Sciences Center, its services extend across the Central Virginia community and beyond—around the world, thanks to the Internet! You'll find lots of information about children's health, from clinical case tutorials, pediatric care, pre-natal health maintenance and immunizations, to a hypertext index of children's diseases and a primer of molecular genetics.

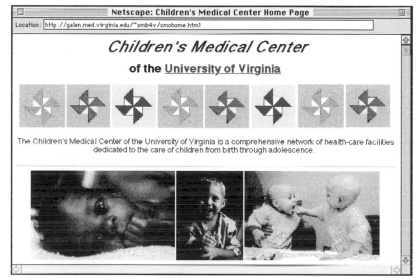

INTEGRATION IDEAS

• Wellness night
Host a combined technology/wellness night. Invite parents and children to use the hands-on, multimedia tutorials at this site to explore what interests them, perhaps asthma, cerebral palsy, diabetes, or ear infections.

• Breathing
Have students use the site to listen to normal breathing compared to asthmatic breathing. Have them listen to each other's breathing and talk about what they heard and what it means.
URL: http://galen.med.virginia.edu/~smb4v/tutorial.html

OTHER SITES RELATED TO THIS TOPIC

Hospital Education for Children
    URL: http://galen.med.virginia.edu/~smb4v/hosped.html
National Institute of Infectious Disease
    URL: gopher://gopher.niaid.nih.gov
Virginia Computerized Children's Immunization Network
    URL: http://galen.med.virginia.edu/~smb4v/immune.html

GLOBAL HEALTH NETWORK

URL: http://info.pitt.edu/HOME/GHNet/GHNet.html

The concept of the Global Health Network (GHN) is simple: Its organizers hope to network everyone engaged in public health and prevention worldwide using the Net! "With telecommunications technology and exciting statistical approaches we can make the monitoring of diseases in many ways similar to the monitoring of the weather," say the organizers. "With health, as with the weather, we know the patterns of diseases in the past and this can be used to accurately predict the future."

INTEGRATION IDEA

● Disease projection
Have students research the status of infectious diseases, such as Ebola outbreaks, AIDS, and tuberculosis. Have them report statistics, projections, and how health officials battle the diseases. The following site links to the current global health situation and projections.
URL: http://www.who.ch/whosis/globest/globest.htm

OTHER SITES RELATED TO THIS TOPIC

AIDS Daily Summaries
    URL: gopher://odie.niaid.nih.gov/11/aids/cdcds
Communicable Disease Surveillance Centre
    URL: http://www.open.gov.uk/cdsc/cdschome.htm
Ebola Home Page
    URL: http://ichiban.objarts.com/ebola/ebola.html

HEALTH EXPLORER

URL: http://hyrax.med.uth.tmc.edu/ptnt/tocptnt.htm

All students in grades eight and up will find helpful information here. They'll find all kinds of basic health information, including tips on diet and exercise, stress, a self-teaching unit about asthma, cancer, and the chicken pox vaccine. More entries are added to the site each month, making this a valuable site to add to your regular lesson plans concerning health.

Netscape: MEDIC: HEALTH EXPLORER

Location: http://hyrax.med.uth.tmc.edu/ptnt/tocptnt.htm

HEALTH EXPLORER

This forum is provided to you by the Health Care Professionals at U.T. Houston. Please understand it is designed to assist you in your understanding of your health and a healthy lifestyle and we encourage you to discuss any topics found here and questions raised through your study of these works with your physician.

Healthy Living

- Diet/Nutrition
- Excercise
- Stress

INTEGRATION IDEA

• Vegetarianism
Have students use the nutrition section to learn about what it means to be a vegetarian. Have them visit the glossary, the area on famous vegans, and other links. Have them build a week-long menu of vegetarian meals.

OTHER SITES RELATED TO THIS TOPIC

Fitness for a Health Heart Lesson
   URL: http://hyrax.med.uth.tmc.edu/ptnt/00000384.htm
Mammography Basics
   URL: http://hyrax.med.uth.tmc.edu/ptnt/00000757.htm
Mini-Medical School Online
   URL: http://hyrax.med.uth.tmc.edu/ptnt/00000382.htm

HEALTHLINKS

URL: http://www.hslib.washington.edu

HealthLinks is an evolving project of the University of Washington and the Health Sciences Libraries and Information Center. Its purpose is to consolidate and distribute electronic health information across the Internet, and to link to selected information available over the Internet. The site includes a large Education component with links to a hands-on biological sciences resource page, genetics and Lyme disease teaching modules, and an interactive Web HyperMuscle exhibit.
URL: http://www.hslib.washington.edu/education/
An intensive, online course of study can be undertaken at this site regarding basic health. All lessons can be obtained from a single Web address.
URL: http://www.hslib.washington.edu/your_health/

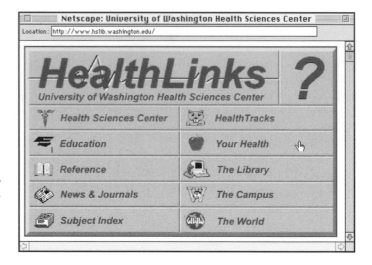

INTEGRATION IDEAS

• Humor helps
Have students click on Health to learn how humor improves health. Have them design and perform programs using humor to brighten the lives of people in hospitals, nursing homes, etc.

• Skating safety
Have students use this site to learn about safety gear for inline skating. They can create a chart or poster showing the types of skating-related injuries and prevention techniques.

OTHER SITES RELATED TO THIS TOPIC

Genetics Online Course
URL: http://oac1.oac.tju.edu/CWIS/OAC/genetics/gcmenu.html
HyperMuscle Exhibit
URL: http://www.med.umich.edu/lrc/hypermuscle/flex.mpg
International Travelers Clinic
URL: http://www.intmed.mcw.edu/travel.html

INTERNATIONAL FOOD INFORMATION COUNCIL

URL: http://ificinfo.health.org

For those teaching or learning about good eating habits, there are few sites better than the International Food Information Council's home on the Web. To promote its goal of helping people worldwide "make informed food choices," the Council has assembled a wealth of information about food safety, nutrition, and health. Follow the Information for Educators link for invaluable teaching aids, including reprints of articles from Food Insight such as "Breakfast: Waking Up to a Healthy Start." The Information for Parents, Information for Consumers, and Food Safety and Nutrition Information sections are loaded with information on topics ranging from food allergies to food advertising and labeling.

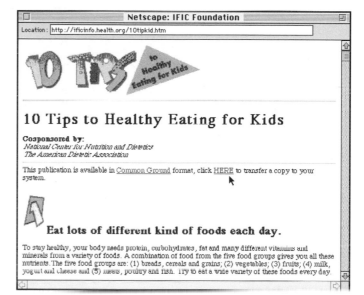

INTEGRATION IDEAS

• Food news
Create a "Food News Team" of students who will periodically visit the IFIC news section to find new information about diet and nutrition, especially as it relates to young people. Have the team regularly prepare a one-page report.

• Commercials
Have students research food advertising and how it affects children's nutrition. Have them compare fun commercials that have positive and negative effects. Have them prepare their own commercials for healthy eating habits.

CONTACT INFORMATION

International Food Information Council
1100 Connecticut Avenue, N.W.
Suite 430
Washington, DC 20036
Email to: foodinfo@ific.health.org

ONCOLINK CANCER RESOURCE CENTER

URL: http://cancer.med.upenn.edu

OncoLink is the first multimedia oncology information resource on the Internet and is freely accessible worldwide to anyone with Internet access. It has the following objectives: dissemination of information relevant to the field of oncology; education of health care personnel; education of patients, families, and students; and rapid collection of information pertinent to cancer.

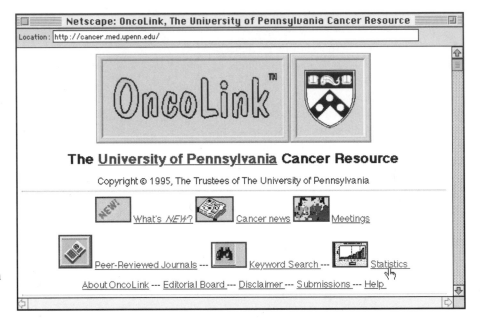

INTEGRATION IDEAS

• Smoking
Have students browse the section on smoking and tobacco. What evidence links smoking to cancer? What do they think of increasing the cigarette tax? What effect would it have on teen smokers?

• Patient art
Students can view a collection of art by children with cancer at the following site.
URL: http://cancer.med.upenn.edu/images/ child/gallery1.html

OTHER SITES RELATED TO THIS TOPIC

CancerGuide
    URL: http://bcn.boulder.co.us/health/cancer/canguide.html
Cancer Support Groups
    URL: http://cancer.med.upenn.edu/stuff/assn_support.html
Cancer Survivor Surveys
    URL: http://cancer.med.upenn.edu/psycho_stuff/survivor.html

SUBSTANCE ABUSE PREVENTION CENTER

URL: http://www.health.org

This Web site is an easily searched, central clearinghouse for substance abuse information. It includes the latest estimates from the Drug Abuse Warning Network, surveys of drug use from around the world, and citizen guides to prevention resources on the Internet.

Netscape: NCADI – National Clearinghouse for Alcohol and Drug Information

Location: http://www.health.org/

Center for Substance Abuse Prevention

PreventionWORKS!

National Clearinghouse for Alcohol and Drug Information

A Service of:

Center for Substance Abuse Prevention
Substance Abuse and Mental Health Services Administration
U. S. Public Health Service
U. S. Department of Health and Human Services

INTEGRATION IDEAS

• Drug awareness
Have students read the site's Prevention Primer, an easily-digestible list of drug terms and prevention techniques. Quiz them on its contents. **URL: http://www.health.org/primer/toc.htm**

• Home use
Students can also read the 1993 National Household Survey on Drug Use at this site. What trends did it reveal? What can be done to curb drug use? **URL: http://www.health.org/hhs/93hhsrvy.htm**

OTHER SITES RELATED TO THIS TOPIC

Canada Center on Substance Abuse
    URL: http://www.ccsa.ca
"Join Together" Substance Abuse Prevention Task Force
    URL: http://www.jointogether.org/jointogether.html
United Nations Internet Drug Control Programme
    URL: http://www.undcp.org

T R A U M A N E T

URL: http://www.trauma.lsumc.edu

While this site will appeal to students interested in becoming doctors or nurses, TraumaNet contains several hands-on lessons involving trauma cases that will enrich any lesson plan on medicine. Each case includes a detailed synopsis, along with an online picture and x-ray history of diagnosis and treatment. This full-featured site is a great showcase of the multimedia capabilities of the Web.

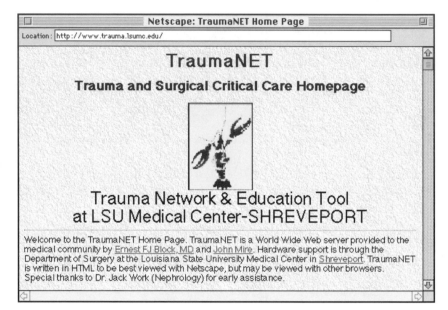

INTEGRATION IDEAS

• Case histories
Have students visit the site each month to review the latest medical case posted to the site.
URL: http://www.trauma.lsumc.edu/ monthlycases.html

• ER life
Have students watch a TV hospital drama. Then, have them use this site to research real-life work in an emergency room situation. How do they compare?

OTHER SITES RELATED TO THIS TOPIC

Emergency Medical Services Home Page
      URL: http://galaxy.einet.net/galaxy/Community/Health/Emergency-Medicine/ fritz-nordengren/ems.html
Injury Control Resource Information Network
      URL: http://info.pitt.edu/~hweiss/injury
TraumaNet Gopher Site
      URL: gopher://www.trauma.lsumc.edu

ART

Anima Media Arts

http://
www.amina.wis.net

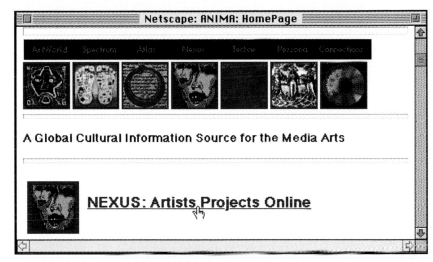

ART

Fractal Movie Archive

http://
www.cnam.fr/
fractals/anim.html

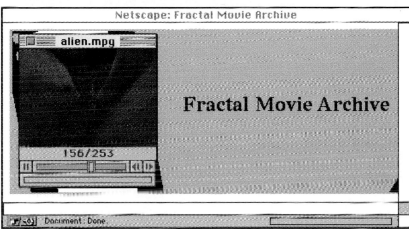

ART

The Louvre

http://
www.emf.net/louvre/

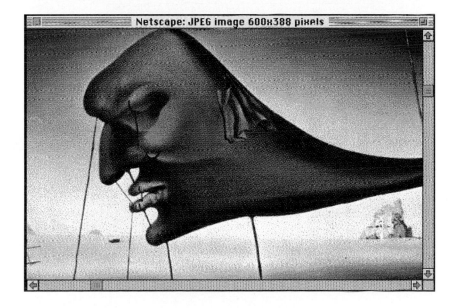

BUSINESS

Radio HK Internet Radio

http://
www.hkweb.com/radio

ENGLISH/LITERATURE

Bartlett's Familiar Passages, Phrases, and Proverbs

http://
www.columbia.edu/~svl2/bartlett/

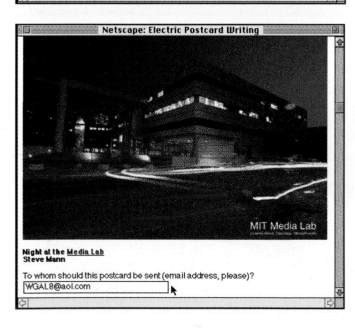

ENGLISH/LITERATURE

The Electric Postcard

http://
postcards.www.media.mit.edu/
Postcards/

ENGLISH/ LITERATURE

The Froggy Page

http://
www.cs.yale.edu/HTML/
YALE/CS/HyPlans/
loosemore-sandra/froggy.html

ENGLISH/ LITERATURE

Online Children's Books

http://
www.digimark.net/iatech/books/

ENGLISH/ LITERATURE

Pathfinder

http://
pathfinder.com

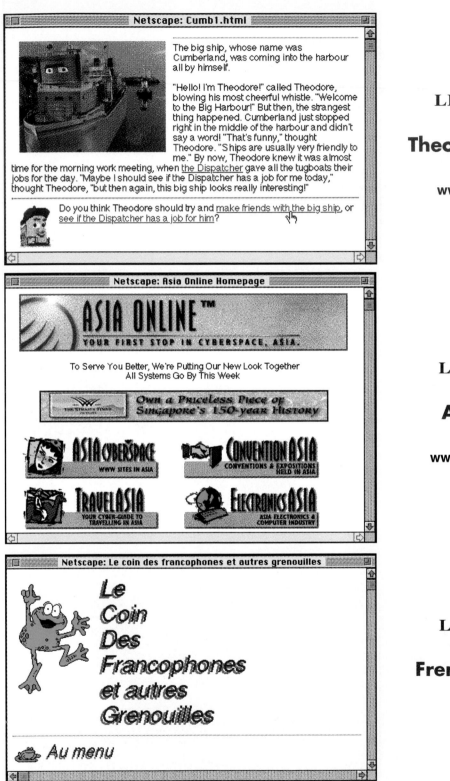

**ENGLISH/
LITERATURE**

Theodore Tugboat

http://
www.cochran.com

**FOREIGN
LANGUAGES**

Asia Online

http://
www.asia-online.com

**FOREIGN
LANGUAGES**

**French Language
Web**

http://
web.cnam.fr/fr/

FOREIGN LANGUAGES

Intercultural E-Mail Classroom Connections

http://
www.stolaf.edu/network/iecc/

Intercultural E-Mail Classroom Connections

The **IECC** (Intercultural E-Mail Connections) mailing lists are provided by St. Olaf College as a free service to help teachers and classes link with partners in other countries and cultures for e-mail classroom pen-pal and project exchanges. Please choose:

- **About using this page**

- How to Subscribe to IECC
- **Submit a request to IECC**
- **Search all IECC Archives**

- **Announcements**
- Related Resources

- Browse IECC-HE
- Browse IECC
- Browse IECC-PROJECTS
- Browse IECC-SURVEYS
- Browse IECC-DISCUSSION

IECC-HE (for Higher Ed)

IECC-HE is intended for teachers seeking partner classrooms for

GEOGRAPHY

European Home Page

http://
s700.uminho.pt/europa.htm

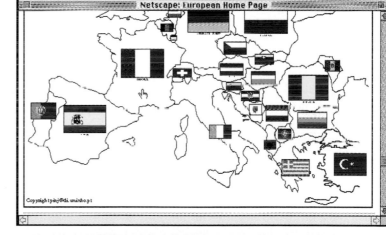

GEOGRAPHY

Virtual Tourist World Map

http://
wings.buffalo.edu/world/

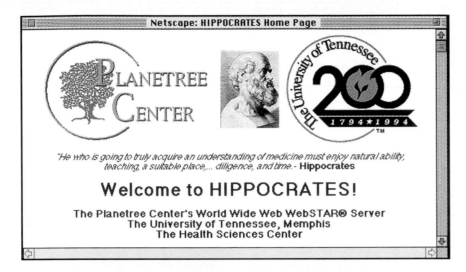

HEALTH/ PHYSICAL EDUCATION

Hippocrates

http:// planetree1.utmem.edu/ Hippocrates.html

HEALTH/ PHYSICAL EDUCATION

International Food Information Council

http:// ificinfo.health.org

HEALTH/ PHYSICAL EDUCATION

National Parent Information Network

http:// ericps.ed.uiuc.edu/ npin/npinhome.html

HISTORY

Anti-Imperialism in the United States, 1898-1935

http://
web.syr.edu/~fjzwick/
ail98-35.html

Netscape: Anti-Imperialism in the United States, 1898-1935

Anti-Imperialism in the United States, 1898-1935

Maintained by Jim Zwick, Syracuse University

Contents

- Imperialists and Anti-Imperialists: The Roots of American Non-Intervention Movements, by Jim Zwick, Syracuse University
- U.S. Racism and Intervention in the Third World, Past and Present, by Daniel B. Schirmer
- The Anti-Imperialist League: A Brief Organizational History
- "The White Man's Burden" and Its Critics
- The American Fund for Public Service Committee on American Imperialism
- The All-America Anti-Imperialist League

HISTORY

Civil War Photographs

http://
rs6.loc.gov/
cwphome.html

Netscape: JPEG image 659x676 pixels

MATHEMATICS

Ask Dr. Math

http://
olmo.swarthmore.edu/
dr-math/dr-math.html

Netscape: Ask Dr. Math!

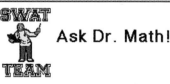

Ask Dr. Math!

We created *Ask Dr. Math* after stumbling on the no-longer functioning *Ask Prof. Maths* program and deciding that this would be a cool project for us to run. We asked a few Swarthmore math students and they were thrilled at the idea. So, we're off and running with many students and even world-famous mathematicians working on The Swat Team to answer K12 student math questions. Elementary and high school students are encouraged to write to **dr.math@forum.swarthmore.edu** for help.

Dr. Math Archives: Questions & Answers

Two convenient ways to access the archives:

Table of Contents -- organized by grade level (elementary, middle school, high school) and topic (exponents, infinity, polynomials, etc.).

Search the archives -- by keyword (decimal, fractal, pi, proof, etc.)

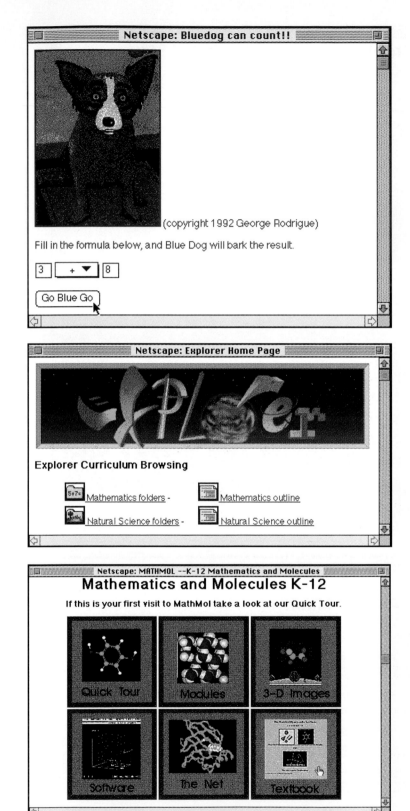

MATHEMATICS

Blue Dog

http://
fedida.ini.cmu.edu:5550/bdf.html

MATHEMATICS

The Explorer

http://
unite2.tisl.ukans.edu

MATHEMATICS

Mathematics & Molecules K-12

http://
www.nyu.edu/pages/mathmol/

MATHEMATICS

MegaMath

http://
www.c3.lanl.gov/
mega-math/welcome.html

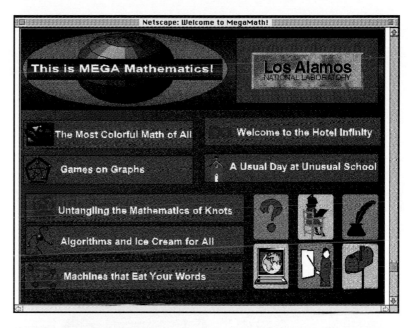

SCIENCE

Centre for Atmospheric Science

http://
www.atm.ch.cam.ac.uk

SCIENCE

CU-SeeMe Internet Videoconferencing Program

http://
cu-seeme.cornell.edu

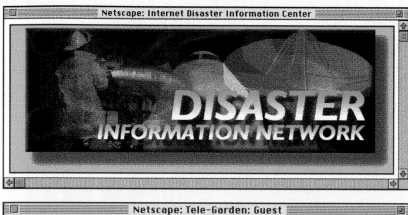

SCIENCE

Internet Disaster Information Network

http://
www.disaster.org

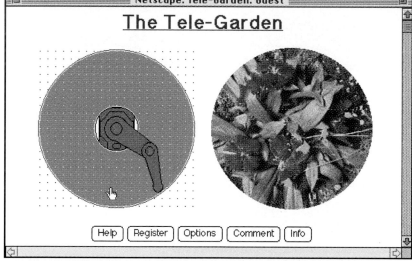

SCIENCE

The Mercury Project Tele-Garden

http://
cwis.usc.edu/dept/garden/

SCIENCE

Missouri Botanical Garden

http://
straylight.tamu.edu/
MoBot/welcome.html

SCIENCE

Museum of Paleontology

http://
ucmp1.berkeley.edu/
exhibittext/entrance.html

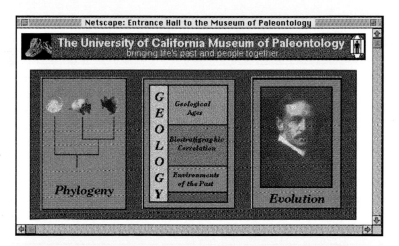

SCIENCE

NASA on the Internet

http://
www.gsfc.nasa.gov/
hqpao/hqpao_home.html

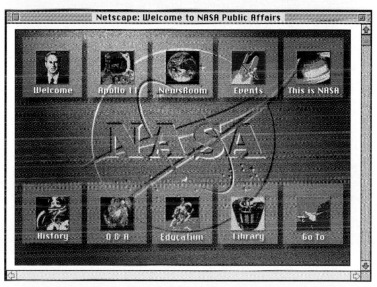

SCIENCE

The Nine Planets Tour

http://
seds.lpl.arizona.edu/billa/tnp/

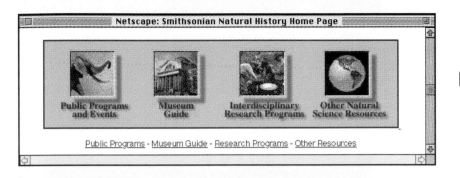

SCIENCE

Smithsonian Natural History Home Page

http://
nmnhwww.si.edu/
nmnhweb.html

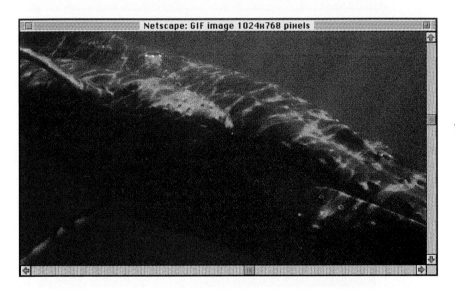

SCIENCE

Whale Watching Web

http://
www.physics.helsinki.fi/
whale/

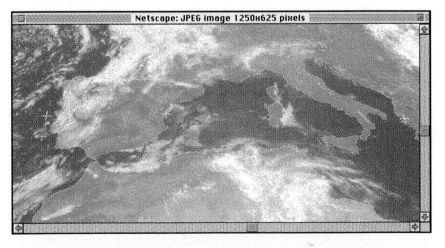

SCIENCE

Virtual Weather Maps & Satellite Images

http://
rs560.cl.msu.edu/
weather/

SCIENCE

Volcano World

http://
volcano.und.nodak.edu

SCIENCE

Netscape: VolcanoWorld Home Page

HOWDY! MY NAME IS ROCKY AND I WANT TO WELCOME YOU TO...

VOLCANO World

Supported by NASA's Program:

Public Use of Earth and Space Science Data Over the Internet

● **What is VolcanoWorld?** Jan 15

SOCIAL SCIENCES/ HUMANITIES

Classroom Connect on the Net

http://
www.wentworth.com

Netscape: Classroom Connect on the Net!

CLASSROOM CONNECT ON THE NET

What's New?

INTRODUCTION   LINKS & SEARCHES

CLASSROOM WEB   CONFERENCE WEB

SEMINARS   PRODUCTS

SOCIAL SCIENCES/ HUMANITIES

EdWeb

http://
k12.cnidr.org:90

Netscape: The EdWeb Home Room

EdWeb   Home Room
Exploring Technology
and School Reform

The K-12 Internet Testbed

This summer, CPB will offer technology grants to as many as a dozen K-12 schools around the U.S. Schools will team up with local public broadcasters to develop new curricula which utilize Internet publishing tools. Unfortunately, the final deadline has already passed, but if you're interest in the project, visit this page to learn more.

**SOCIAL SCIENCES/
HUMANITIES**

**ERIC Educator
Resources on the
Web**

http://
eryx.syr.edu

Reproduction of the FBI seal is prohibited under Title 18, United States Code, Section 701, and Title 41, Code of Federal Regulations, Section 128–1.5007.

**SOCIAL SCIENCES/
HUMANITIES**

**Federal Bureau of
Investigation (FBI)**

http://
naic.nasa.gov/fbi/
FBI_homepage.html

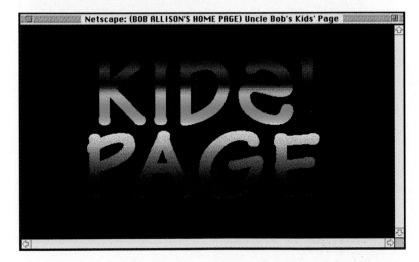

**SOCIAL SCIENCES/
HUMANITIES**

Kids' Page

http://
gagme.wwa.com/
~boba/kidsi.html

SOCIAL SCIENCES/
HUMANITIES

National Public Radio

http://
www.npr.org

SOCIAL
SCIENCES/HUMANITIES

White House Web

http://
www.whitehouse.gov

SOCIAL SCIENCES/
HUMANITIES

Wired

http://
www.wired.com

VOCATIONAL EDUCATION

CareerMosaic

http://
www.careermosaic.com

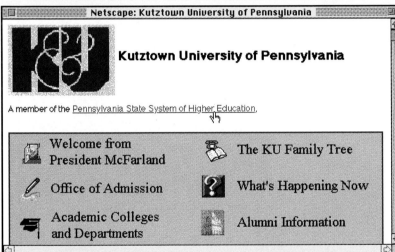

VOCATIONAL EDUCATION

Directory of American Universities & Colleges

http://
www.clas.ufl.edu/CLAS/
american-universities.html

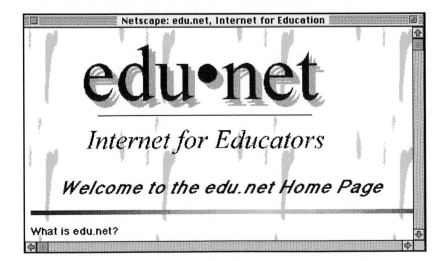

VOCATIONAL EDUCATION

Edu.Net

http://
www.execpc.com/~jlk/

U.S. HEALTH STATISTICS

URL: http://www.cdc.gov/nchswww/nchshome.htm

What is the relationship between cigarette smoking and other unhealthy behaviors among U.S. youth? What are the latest statistics on contraceptive use, or office visits for glaucoma? All of these questions and more are answered here at the National Centers for Disease Control and Prevention's online health statistics Web site.

INTEGRATION IDEA

• Research

As students research a health topic, require them to use this site to add the most recent statistics and research. Two Web pages contain the latest research:
URL: http://www.cdc.gov/nchswww/95facts.htm
URL: http://www.cdc.gov/nchswww/94facts.htm

OTHER SITES RELATED TO THIS TOPIC

Centers for Disease Control and Prevention Home Page
      URL: http://www.cdc.gov/cdc.html
National Institutes of Health
      URL: http://www.nih.gov
National Library of Medicine
      URL: http://www.nlm.nih.gov/welcome.html

VIRTUAL HOSPITAL

URL: http://indy.radiology.uiowa.edu

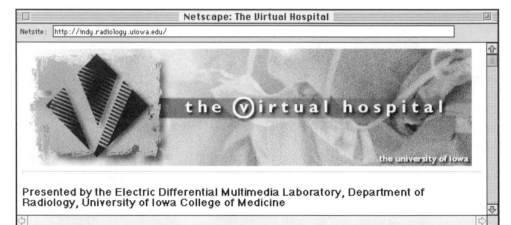

The Virtual Hospital (VH) is a continuously updated medical multimedia database that can be accessed through high speed networks 24 hours a day. The VH provides invaluable patient care support and distance learning to practicing physicians and will be of great interest to students considering a career in medicine. The site puts the latest medical information at physicians' fingertips and is an aid in answering patient care questions. Its multimedia textbooks offer functions such as free text searching, the ability to play video and audio clips, and the opportunity to display an unlimited number of high-resolution images.

INTEGRATION IDEA

• Pre-med explorations
Have students access and review the site's online multimedia textbooks. Current titles include Lung Anatomy, Lung Disease, Joint Fluoroscopy, Muscle Injuries, Back Pain, and Pediatric Airway Disease.
URL: http://indy.radiology.uiowa.edu/Providers/Textbooks/MultimediaTextbooks.html

OTHER SITES RELATED TO THIS TOPIC

History of Medicine
        URL: http://www.nlm.nih.gov/hmd.dir/hmd.html
Online Medical Teaching Files
        URL: http://indy.radiology.uiowa.edu/Providers/TeachingFiles/MultimediaTeachingFiles.html
Virtual Medical Patient Simulations
        URL: http://indy.radiology.uiowa.edu/Providers/Simulations/PatientSimulations.html

WOMEN'S HEALTH HOT LINE HOME PAGE

URL: http://www.soft-design.com/softinfo/womens-health.html

This Web site's design is devoid of fancy graphics or flashing lights, but it offers plenty of authoritative and user-friendly material. Each monthly issue of this valuable online newsletter goes in-depth on health topics important to women. Past issues focused on topics such as "How to evaluate confusing medical news" and "Beating the top killer of women" (heart disease).

INTEGRATION IDEA

● **Health myths**

Divide the class into groups and instruct them to look for information for compiling a women's health "Myth Buster" report that proves common misconceptions to be false, such as the belief that women don't have to worry about heart attacks.

OTHER SITES RELATED TO THIS TOPIC

Breast Cancer Information Clearinghouse
URL: http://nysernet.org/breast/Default.html
Community Breast Health Project
URL: http://www-med.stanford.edu:80/CBHP/
Self Breast Examination & Mammography
URL: http://www.net-advisor.com/mammog/

CHAPTER 7

HISTORY

1492 EXHIBIT

URL: http://sunsite.unc.edu/expo/1492.exhibit/Intro.html

"Columbus. 1492. The date and the name provoke many questions related to the linking of very different parts of the world, the Western Hemisphere and the Mediterranean. What was life like in those areas before 1492? How did European, African, and American peoples react to each other?" This site, called 1492: An Ongoing Voyage, is based on an exhibit at the Library of Congress. It's a fine introduction to the richness and diversity of native societies of the American continents *before* contact with Europeans. The

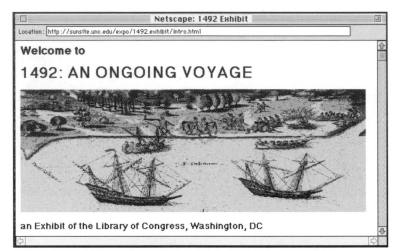

exhibit also describes the Mediterranean culture of the time and the effect of the resulting clash of the two cultures. Displays range from the ruins at Machu Picchu to the first map of California. An outline gives a quick overview of objects in the exhibit, which is divided into six sections. This is a fine example of how students can visit museums without leaving their desks.

INTEGRATION IDEAS

• Role playing
Have groups of students choose one of the native societies or a Mediterranean society. Have students research, then role play their group and perform a skit or make a multimedia presentation presenting 1492 from its point of view.

• Achievements
Have students do in-depth research of the native societies of the Americas. Have them report on the achievements of each, including specific examples. Which of these achievements became major contributions to human progress?

OTHER SITES RELATED TO THIS TOPIC

Art (1492 Art Exhibit)
> **URL: http://sunsite.unc.edu/expo/1492.exhibit/overview.html**

Christopher Columbus Links
> **URL: gopher://sundns.millersv.edu/11/other/columbus**

Columbus' Home Town in Sweden
> **URL: http://www.csd.uu.se/uppsala-student/uppsalaguide/guide.html**

AMERICAN CIVIL WAR INFORMATION ARCHIVE

URL: http://www.access.digex.net/~bdboyle/cw.html

This Web page is your jumping-off point to everything the Internet has to offer about the American Civil War. Visit the Civil War Archive at the Library of Congress, review online Civil War documents, find out where to attend reenactment and living history museums, look over detailed regimental histories, and walk through the National Museum of Civil War Medicine.

Netscape: civil War Information, Documents, and Archive

Location: http://www.access.digex.net/~bdboyle/cw.html

The American Civil War, 1861-1865

INTEGRATION IDEAS

• Online critique
Have students compare and contrast the information at this site. Evaluate the archives, databases, and homepages for structure, content, organization, and interest level. What makes a good online resource? Do graphics enhance or detract from readability? Is print material easy to read?

• Battle plans
Have students use this site to review the orders of battle for major engagements. Where were the hot spots? Which battles were turning points in the war?

OTHER SITES RELATED TO THIS TOPIC

American Civil War Page at the University of Tennessee
URL: http://cobweb.utcc.utk.edu/~hoemann/warweb.html
Letters Home from a Soldier in the U.S. Civil War
URL: http://www.ucsc.edu/civil-war-letters/home.html
National Cryptologic Museum
URL: http://www.nsa.gov:8080/museum/tour.html

ANCIENT NEAR EAST STUDIES

URL: http://www-oi.uchicago.edu:80/OI/DEPT/RA/ABZU/ABZU.HTML

Did you know that the ancient Egyptians recycled papyrus in their "offices," much like we recycle paper today? There's one difference though—they used recycled papyrus for mummification! That's just one of the interesting tidbits students can find at ABZU, an experimental, comprehensive guide to the rapidly increasing data relevant to the study of the Ancient Near East. Your students will find links to museum collections, an index of resources by region (Egypt or Mesopotamia), online archeological sites and data, and library catalogs and journals. Anyone doing research on the Ancient Near East should make this their first online stop.

INTEGRATION IDEAS

• Papyrus
Have students use this site's dozens of links to the latest information about papyrus—how it was made, remaining fragments, and museum collections—and write a report or make a presentation.
URL: http://odyssey.lib.duke.edu:80/papyrus/
URL: http://www-oi.uchicago.edu:80/OI/DEPT/RA/ABZU/ABZU_REGINDX_EGYPT_PAP.HTML

• Scavenger hunt
Have students work in teams and use this site to formulate questions for an Ancient Near East Archaeology Scavenger Hunt. Have them exchange questions and go online to dig out the answers.

OTHER SITES RELATED TO THIS TOPIC

3-D Reconstruction of Ancient Egyptian Mummy
> **URL: http://www.pavilion.co.uk/HealthServices/BrightonHealthCare/mummy.htm**

Ancient Near East Academic Journals
> **URL: http://www-oi.uchicago.edu:80/OI/DEPT/RA/ABZU/ABZU_JOURNAL_INDEX.HTML**

Archaeological Sites in Mesopotamia
> **URL: http://www-oi.uchicago.edu:80/OI/DEPT/RA/ABZU/ABZU_REGINDX_MESO.HTML**

BIOGRAPHICAL DICTIONARY

URL:
http://www.mit.edu:8001/afs/athena/activity/c/collegebowl/biog_dict/intro.html

This is the homepage for a biographical reference dictionary. It attempts to present, in a concise format, the basic facts about 16,000 notable figures from ancient times to the present day. A truly interactive, easy-to-search site that younger students will love to use as a research tool.

Netscape: Biographical Dictionary
Location: http://www.mit.edu:8001/afs/athena/user/g/a/galileo/Public/WWW/galileo.html

The files themselves

Aalto-Azzem

Baade-Byron

Caamano-Czolgosz

Daar-Dzerzhinsky

Eads-Ezzelino

Faber-Fyodorov

Gable-Gyongyosi

Haakon-Hypatia

Iacocca-Izvolski

Jabotinsky-Juxon

Kaahumanu-Kyprianou

INTEGRATION IDEA

• Electronic research
During your normal course of study on a particular historical figure, have your students visit this site to enrich their studies about him or her. What new things did they learn at the site?

OTHER SITES RELATED TO THIS TOPIC

American Memory Historical Collection
URL: http://rs6.loc.gov/amhome.html
Biographical Initiative
URL: http://www.mdarchives.state.md.us/msa/homepage/html/educ.html
Historical and Literary Graphics
URL: http://web.syr.edu/~fjzwick/graphics.html

ELECTRIC RENAISSANCE ONLINE COURSE

URL: http://www.idbsu.edu:80/courses/hy309/

While originally created for students at Boise State University, this Web site contains a free, universally-available college course on the Renaissance that anyone may participate in. The subject matter of the course is the history of Europe from roughly 1300 to 1500. The emphasis is on Italy, especially the Italian Renaissance, but events north of the Alps are covered as well. Your high school history students will enjoy the in-depth material and may even join in live, online discussions with students at Boise State. You can easily change any of the lessons and assignments to fit any high school history curriculum.

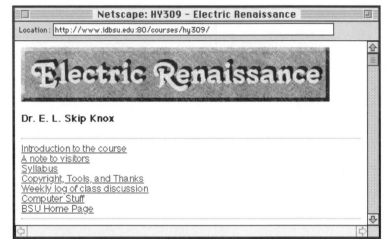

INTEGRATION IDEAS

• Diplomatic reports

Have students pick a city or state and write a brief report each week from the point of view of a diplomat living in the region. For instance, a diplomat from Florence would report to the signoria on political conditions, economic trends, societal developments, etc.

• Distance learning

Have students compare and contrast electronic courses with live courses. What are the advantages and disadvantages of taking a course via telecommunications?

OTHER SITES RELATED TO THIS TOPIC

Botticelli Exhibit
    URL: http://sunsite.unc.edu/louvre/paint/auth/botticelli/
Maps of Florence and France during the Renaissance
    URL: http://www.idbsu.edu:80/courses/hy309/maps/maps.html
Michelangelo Exhibit
    URL: http://sunsite.unc.edu/louvre/paint/auth/michelangelo/

HISTORY OF CHINA

URL: http://darkwing.uorcgon.cdu/~fclsing/cstuff/history.html

Links to hundreds of online databases with information about China, including its history, can be found at this site. Among its features arc the extensive Lishi Yanjiu Asia Library, chronologies of Chinese history, sound bites and full-texts from Mao Zedong's library, information on Five-ycar Projects, many works related to the democracy movement, and much more. One link takes you to a comprehensive index to the entire site.
URL: http://darkwing.uoregon.edu/ ~felsing/cstuff/cshelf.html

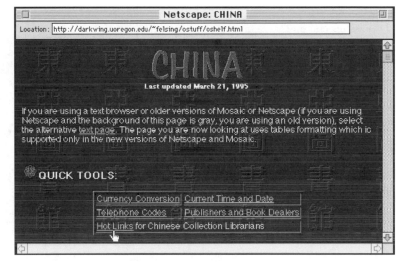

INTEGRATION IDEAS

• Democracy movement
Assign groups of students a document from the Democracy Movement section. Have them study the language, assertions, testimony, reasoning, demands, fears, and concerns in the documents. How do these writings compare with similar writings, such as the Declaration of Independence?

• Timeline
Using information from the site, have students construct a detailed wall chart (or a multimedia presentation) of Chinese history, complete with illustrations.

OTHER SITES RELATED TO THIS TOPIC
Beijing Massacre Anniversary Home Page
    URL: http://darkwing.uoregon.edu/~felsing/cstuff/cndspec.html
Chinese History Chronology
    URL: http://www.cernet.edu.cn/history.html
History of Chinese Mathematics
    URL: http://aleph0.clarku.edu/~djoyce/mathhist/china.htm

LIBRARY OF CONGRESS SOVIET ARCHIVES

URL: http://sunsite.unc.edu:80/pjones/russian/Soviet_Archive_Introduction.html

The documents in this exhibit at the Library of Congress provide an unprecedented inside look at the workings of one of the largest, most powerful, and long-lived political machines of the modern era—the Soviet government. They cover the entire range of Soviet history, from the October Revolution of 1917 to the failed coup of August 1991, and include material from archives that had been key working files of the Communist rulers until August 1991: the archives of the Central Committee, the Presidential archive, and the KGB.

Netscape: GIF image 640x480 pixels

Location: http://sunsite.unc.edu/pjones/russian/pics/gorby1.gif

INTEGRATION IDEAS

• U.S.-U.S.S.R. relations
Have students use online documents to explain relations between the U.S. and U.S.S.R. for the past 80 years, documenting the cooperative and confrontational periods.

• *Communist Manifesto*
Have students compare the manifesto with the U.S. Constitution. Have them use a keyword search to find key words and phrases, such as "liberty," "property," and "rights" and discuss the tone, language, and euphemisms in these political writings.

OTHER SITES RELATED TO THIS TOPIC

Soviet History Newsgroups
> **URL: news:soc.culture.soviet**
> **URL: news:talk.politics.soviet**

General History Resources
> **URL: telnet://hnsource.cc.ukans.edu**

Social Sciences/Humanities (Soviet Anti-Religious Campaigns)
> **URL: http://sunsite.unc.edu:80/pjones/russian/Anti-Religious_Campaigns.html**

Science (Soviet Nuclear Power Program/Chernobyl)
> **URL: http://sunsite.unc.edu:80/pjones/russian/Chernobyl.html**

MILITARY HISTORY

URL: http://kuhttp.cc.ukans.edu:80/history/milhst/m_index.html

The Mil-Hist Home Page is your jumping-off point to hundreds of Internet sites with chronologies and information related to military history. From Ancient & Medieval, to Pre-Twentieth and Twentieth Century, this site links you to online databases concerning everything from the Napoleonic Wars to World War I, II, Vietnam, and the Gulf War. Students studying any armed conflict will find plenty of relevant information.

INTEGRATION IDEAS

• Military hardware

Have students create a timeline of military weaponry and equipment, from medieval catapults to heat-seeking missiles. Which inventions were adopted for peacetime use, e.g., radio, radar, barbed wire, Saturn V rocket?

• Compare and contrast

Have students compare wars and battles from the American Revolution to Desert Storm. Provide questions to guide their research. How did they differ in goals, strategies, and magnitude? How did the development of mass media affect the way wars were fought or supported?

OTHER SITES RELATED TO THIS TOPIC

Air Force Online Image Bank
    URL: http://infosphere.safb.af.mil/~ccam/comcam1.htm
Army Area Handbooks
    URL: gopher://UMSLVMA.UMSL.EDU:70/11/LIBRARY/STACKS/BOOKS/ARMYAHBS
Voice of America Transcripts
    URL: gopher://ftp.voa.gov/11/newswire

THE LABYRINTH

URL: http://www.georgetown.edu:80/labyrinth/labyrinth-home.html

The Labyrinth is a global information network providing free, organized access to electronic resources in medieval studies through a World Wide Web server at Georgetown University. The Labyrinth's easy-to-use menus and hypertext links provide automatic connections to databases, services, and electronic texts on other servers around the world. This site is valuable for your "across the curriculum" lesson plans because it features medieval works written in Latin, Italian, and Middle English by authors such as Virgil, Dante, and Chaucer, respectively. Follow this link: **URL: http://www.georgetown.edu/labyrinth/ library/library.html**
You'll also find more than 20 hands-on, medieval history lesson plans and activities at the site. **URL: http://www.georgetown.edu/labyrinth/pedagogical/pedagog.html**

INTEGRATION IDEAS

• **Web as myth**
Have students read the section on Ariadne's Thread and the Labyrinth in the Classical Mythology section to see how navigating the World Wide Web is similar to how Thesus went through the Labyrinth.

• **Camelot studies**
Have students browse the Resources for Arthurian Studies section and do research to separate historical fact from legend. Why are Arthurian and medieval stories, movies, and games, popular today?

OTHER SITES RELATED TO THIS TOPIC

Institute of Historical Research, London
     URL: http://ihr.sas.ac.uk:8080/ihr/ihr0101.html
Internet Discussion Lists for Students of History
     URL: gopher://ukanaix.cc.ukans.edu:70/11/hnsource/H-Net_news/Lists
Online Latin Texts
     URL: http://ukanaix.cc.ukans.edu:80/ftp/pub/history/Europe/Medieval/latintexts/

TREASURES OF THE CZARS

URL: http://www.times.st-pete.fl.us/treasures/TC.Lobby.html

You and your class could fly to Florida's International Museum to see its breathtaking Treasures of the Czars exhibition, or you could save your time and pennies and view it here. The Treasures are more than 250 items from the reign of the Romanov czars (1613 to 1917). Those centuries were a period of monumental change in Russia: from a church-dominated, insular land to a secular, militaristic member of the European council of nations. This exhibit is said to be the largest collection of items ever sent out of the country by the Moscow Kremlin Museums. You'll also find eight separate lesson plan ideas using information on the site. Go to the following location.
URL: http://www.times.st-pete.fl.us/treasures/TC.5.a.4.html

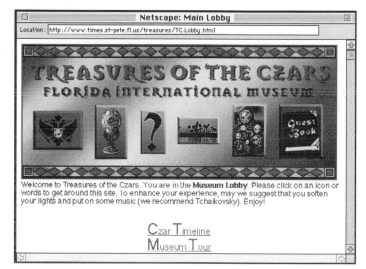

INTEGRATION IDEAS

• Journal exchange

Have your students tour this site and keep a journal of their virtual field trip. Find a keypal class in St. Petersburg, Florida, which has physically visited the exhibit, and have the classes exchange their journals. Are they noticeably different?

• Two St. Petersburgs

Have students search the entire Web to write essays on the differences and similarities between the sister cities in Florida and Russia. Start at A Tale of Two St. Petersburgs at the following site.
URL: http://www.times.st-pete.fl.us/ Treasures2/TC.4.5.html

OTHER SITES RELATED TO THIS TOPIC

Art (History)
    URL: http://rubens.anu.edu.au
Art (News)
    URL: news:clari.news.arts
Art (Soviet Art)
    URL: http://www.times.st-pete.fl.us/treasures/TC.2.1.html

UNITED STATES HOLOCAUST MEMORIAL MUSEUM

URL: http://www.ushmm.org:80/index.html

Students studying this grim period of human history will find the museum's Web site to be a valuable information storehouse for many Holocaust-related resources, as well as an online kiosk for visitors information. As the site states: "The mission of the United States Holocaust Memorial Museum is to present the facts of the Holocaust, to tell the American public as clearly and comprehensively as possible what happened in that dark chapter of human history. To this end, the Museum has

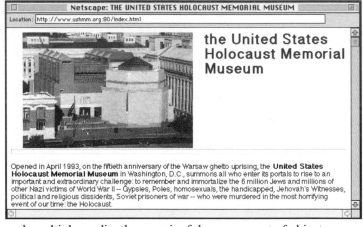

Opened in April 1993, on the fiftieth anniversary of the Warsaw ghetto uprising, the **United States Holocaust Memorial Museum** in Washington, D.C., summons all who enter its portals to rise to an important and extraordinary challenge: to remember and immortalize the 6 million Jews and millions of other Nazi victims of World War II -- Gypsies, Poles, homosexuals, the handicapped, Jehovah's Witnesses, political and religious dissidents, Soviet prisoners of war -- who were murdered in the most horrifying event of our time: the Holocaust.

reconstructed the history of the Holocaust through multiple media: the meaningful arrangement of objects as well as the presentation of documentary photographic and cinematographic materials." The site also has an in-depth Teaching Manual to the Holocaust at the following location.
URL: http://www.ushmm.org:80/education/ed.html

INTEGRATION IDEAS

• Impersonation
Have students use the site to research the lives of Jewish children in the ghettos and camps of the Holocaust. Have them work with another class online to do an impersonation of a child or children of the time, with one class asking questions and another answering.

• Vocabulary words
Have students read the Frequently Asked Questions section and compile and research related vocabulary words. They can work on unfamiliar words such as "Nazi" and words with new meanings, such as "exterminate," and "cleanse."

OTHER SITES RELATED TO THIS TOPIC

Anti-Semitism and the Holocaust & Holocaust Denial
URL: http://www.ed.ac.uk/~p92002/anti_sem.html
Cybrary of the Holocaust
URL: http://www.pinsight.com/~write/cybrary/index.html
Holocaust Timeline
URL: http://www.kaiwan.com/~greg.ihr/misc/timeline.html

WORLD HISTORY ARCHIVES

URL: http://neal.ctstateu.edu:80/history/world_history/archives/archives.html

Whatever your period of interest, this site provides links to more than 500 online databases containing information about world history. Among its features are documentary archives, online mailing lists about history, lists of history departments at the world's colleges and universities, general history reference works, tools, libraries, and much more.

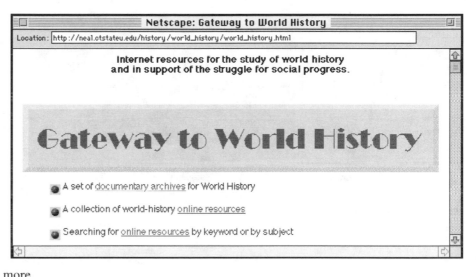

INTEGRATION IDEAS

• Local history
After students have browsed this site extensively, have them plan a hyperlinked Web site depicting their own area's history. It could provide links to local colleges, museums, historical societies, etc. A local provider may even consider mounting it on the Web.

• Ask a historian
As students write a report on world history, require them to go online and submit theoretical or subjective questions to historians.

OTHER SITES RELATED TO THIS TOPIC

African Studies Archives
> **URL: http://neal.ctstateu.edu/history/world_history/archives/afrstud.html**

Marx & Engels Online Library
> **URL: gopher://csf.Colorado.EDU/11/psn/Marx**

NativeWeb
> **URL: http://kuhttp.cc.ukans.edu/~marc/native_main.html**

WORLD OF VIKINGS

URL: http://www.demon.co.uk:80/history/index.html

From current research projects and educational resources to museums and online mailing lists, this site is sure to be a favorite place for any student studying Vikings. You will find a hands-on Viking Unit for young students at the following address:
URL: http://odin.nls.no/ viking/ehome.htm

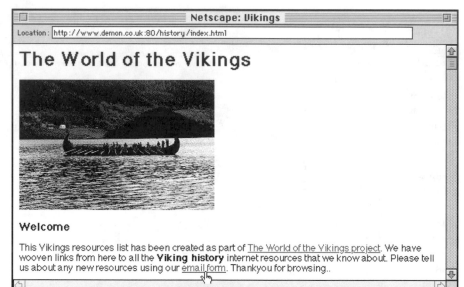

INTEGRATION IDEAS

• Viking quiz
As students complete their study of Vikings, have them go to the following site to tackle the Viking Quiz and see who finishes in the shortest time period.
URL: http://odin.nls.no/viking/equiz.htm

• Good/bad Vikings
Have students use this site to compile a list of the positive (navigation techniques) and negative (raids) contributions of the Vikings. Compare myths about Vikings to historical fact.

OTHER SITES RELATED TO THIS TOPIC

Sigtuna Viking Museum
     URL: http://control.chalmers.se/vikings/viking.html
Viking Navy Home Port
     URL: http://www.digalog.com/peter/viknavy/vikhome.htm
Viking Network Home Page
     URL: http://odin.nls.no/viking/vnethome.htm

MATHEMATICS

BIG SKY TELEGRAPH MATH LESSON PLANS

URL: gopher://bvsd.k12.co.us:70/11/Educational_Resources/Lesson_Plans/

Math teachers should have a field day with this site, which features dozens of online lesson plans on a variety of math subjects. Try "Making Change: Buying at a community store," a lesson for grades K-2 that helps students count how much money they have, determine prices while shopping, and count out the exact change. Or scroll down to find a plan for grade 9 through 12 students called "Significant

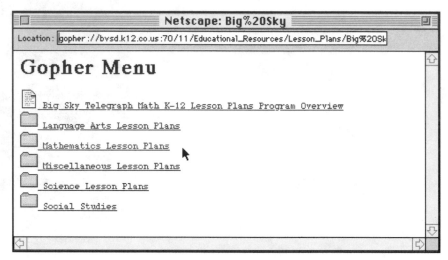

Figures," an activity designed to help students "explore and truly understand which digits are significant when dealing with numbers that represent measured values." Whew! This gopher site contains a single file describing each lesson plan, the individual text documents for each one, and a zipped file containing all of the files together.

INTEGRATION IDEA

• Lesson plans
Scan the list of lesson plans to find those appropriate for your students' grade and competency levels. Download, save to disk, or print them and incorporate them into your current curriculum. Modify these plans to suit your needs or incorporate online components based on other resources in this book.

OTHER SITES RELATED TO THIS TOPIC

Classes You Can Teach Using the Internet
> **URL: gopher://quest.arc.nasa.gov:70/11/**

Eisenhower National Clearinghouse Catalog of Math Curriculum Resources
> **URL: gopher://enc.org**

Math Lesson Plans at ERIC
> **URL: gopher://ericir.syr.edu:70/11/Lesson/Math**

BLUE DOG

URL: http://fedida.ini.cmu.edu:5550/bdf.html

Blue Dog is a friendly, intelligent dog waiting for you on the World Wide Web! Fill in any basic math equation (like 1+1 or 12-10) and Blue will bark the result through your computer's speaker. A fun way to teach young students basic math and counting skills. *Ruff!*

Netscape: Bluedog can count!!

Location: http://fedida.ini.cmu.edu:5550/bdf.html

(copyright 1992 George Rodrigue)

Fill in the formula below, and Blue Dog will bark the result.

| 1 | + ▼ | 5 |

Go Blue Go

INTEGRATION IDEA

● Math practice

After you've taught your K-2 students the basics of counting, allow them to visit this site and have fun practicing their skills with Blue Dog.

OTHER SITES RELATED TO THIS TOPIC

Math Software for Young Students (Mac)
> **URL: http://www-leland.stanford.edu/~lefig/index.html**

Bullfrog Math Software (Mac)
> **URL: ftp://mirrors.aol.com/pub/info-mac/app/edu/bullfrog-math.hqx**

Math Software (Mac & Windows)
> **URL: http://www.yahoo.com/Computers/Software/Mathematics/**

THE EXPLORER

URL: http://unite2.tisl.ukans.edu

The Explorer Home Page, supported in part by the U.S. Department of Education, is one of the richest on the World Wide Web for math educators. Teachers will find pointers to all sorts of valuable math lesson plans, courseware programs, shareware educational games, and videos covering a wide range of curriculum types and grade levels. Many of the resources are free—you can even download software and other materials right to your desktop. Each entry in the Explorer contains detailed information, including a description, objectives and process skills, and the resource's recommended curriculum applications. You can browse folders for information by topic or view the entire contents via hyperlinked index.

Netscape: Explorer Home Page

Location: http://unite2.tisl.ukans.edu/

Explorer Curriculum Browsing

Mathematics folders -

Natural Science folders -

Mathematics outline

Natural Science outline

INTEGRATION IDEAS

• Math activities
Download and use lesson plans and project outlines from this site. Or let students download some of the educational programs and games and try them out.

• Math projects
For a special project, have students bring their math skills to bear by designing their own math lesson plans or projects, or by developing ideas for math software.

OTHER SITES RELATED TO THIS TOPIC

Windows Math Education Software
    URL: ftp://oak.oakland.edu/simtel/win3/math/
DOS Math Education Shareware
    URL: ftp://oak.oakland.edu/simtel/msdos/math/
Macintosh Math Education Software
    URL: gopher://gopher.archive.umich.edu:7055/11/mac/misc/math

GEOMETRY CENTER

URL: http://www.gcom.umn.edu

The Geometry Center is a mathematics research and education center at the University of Minnesota. The Center supports math and computer science research, mathematical visualization, software development, application development, video animation production, and, most importantly, *K-16 math education*. This site contains more than a half-dozen ideas concerning teaching geometry in the classroom. A World Wide Web self-guided tour of the Center's offerings is available—follow the Information for People at the Center link and select Self-Guided Tours.

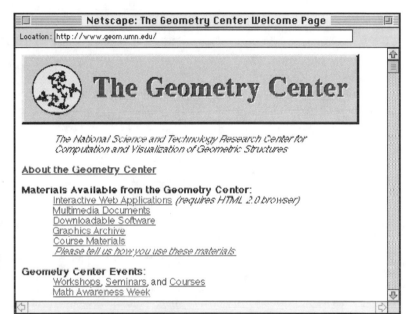

INTEGRATION IDEAS

● Geometric art

Have students visit the graphics archive. Have an artist view the images with the class and discuss how mathematics (especially geometry) and art are related.

● Lesson plans

The site's Geometry Educational Materials Web has six hands-on lesson ideas.
URL: http://www.geom.umn.edu/docs/

OTHER SITES RELATED TO THIS TOPIC

Calculus Online Resources
> **URL: gopher://archives.math.utk.edu:70/11/teaching.materials/calculus.resources**

Graphics Calculators Teaching Materials
> **URL: gopher://archives.math.utk.edu:70/11/teaching.materials/calculator**

Mathematics Archive Gopher
> **URL: gopher://archives.math.utk.edu**

THE HUB

URL: http://hub.terc.edu

The Hub is an Internet resource for mathematics and science education funded by the Eisenhower Regional Consortia and operated on behalf of the Regional Alliance for Mathematics and Science Education Reform. The site's goal is "to transform the technological potential of recent developments in telecommunications into valuable services for policy-makers, educators, administrators, and students in the United States." The

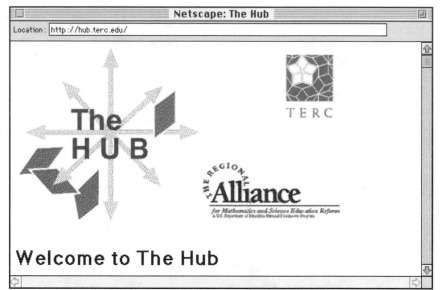

Welcome to The Hub

Hub acts as a central repository of information and links to math-related online resources. It features links to more than 2,000 lesson plans, online projects for students, and hands-on materials to help educators teach their students about discrete mathematics.

INTEGRATION IDEA

• Lesson plans

Hundreds of lesson plans using online math resources are available though hyperlinks here. Start with the Math Curriculum and Projects page by clicking on the Mathematics icon on the home page. Download them to use in your class or to get ideas for creating new lesson plans.

OTHER SITES RELATED TO THIS TOPIC

Science (General Science Curriculum & Projects)
URL: http://hub.terc.edu/physics.html
URL: http://hub.terc.edu:70/1/hub/science/sci_cur

INTERNET CENTER FOR MATHEMATICS PROBLEMS

URL: http://www.mathpro.com/math/mathCenter.html

This site will keep even the most advanced math, algebra, and geometry students busy tackling tough problems online. The goal of the site is to "identify and list all sources of mathematics problems on the Internet," and it certainly appears as if the site designers reached that goal. You'll find hyperlinks such as Problem Columns from Mathematics Journals, Peter Wang's Problem of the Month, and the MathMess Problem of the Week.

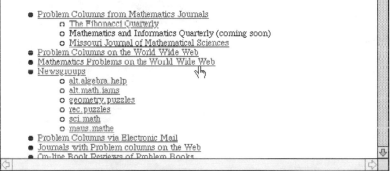

INTEGRATION IDEAS

• Make a problem
After students try some of the problems, have them create their own problems or puzzles and post them to the appropriate newsgroups or Web sites. They could also exchange problems via email with a partner class.

• Guestbook survey
Browse through the online Guestbook and view the comments from teachers around the world. What do they reveal about the Internet's potential?

OTHER SITES RELATED TO THIS TOPIC

Archive of math, cryptology, geometry, and other puzzles
URL: ftp://rtfm.mit.edu/pub/usenet/news.answers/puzzles/archive
Ask Dr. Math!
URL: http://olmo.swarthmore.edu/dr-math/dr-math.html
Electronic Games for Education in Math and Science
URL: http://www.cs.ubc.ca/nest/egems/home.html

MACTUTOR HISTORY OF MATHEMATICS ARCHIVE

URL: http://www-groups.dcs.st-and.ac.uk:80/~history/

Students and teachers of math history, add this site to your hotlist right away. Developed by the St. Andrews School of Mathematics and Computational Sciences, the MacTutor History Archive contains biographies of thousands of important figures in math history, many including photographs that put a human face behind the math masters. The biographies are conveniently indexed with

```
┌─────────────────────────────────────────────────────────────────────┐
│ ▦         Netscape: Short Biographies: Hei              ▦ │
├─────────────────────────────────────────────────────────────────────┤
│ Location: │http://www-groups.dcs.st-and.ac.uk:80/~history/ShortBiogs/Hei.html#Hermann│
├─────────────────────────────────────────────────────────────────────┤
│ Helmholtz, Hermann Ludwig Ferdinand von                               │
│                                                                       │
│ 31 Aug 1821 - 8 Sept 1894                                             │
│ German                                                                │
│ In 1858 he became professor of anatomy and physiology at Bonn, the    │
│ in 1871, professor of physics at Berlin. His most important work was  │
│ in mathematical physics and acoustics where his major study of 1863   │
│ was interested in musical theory and the perception of sound. In      │
│ mathematical appendices he advocated the use of Fourier series. He    │
│ published an important paper on the first law of thermodynamics in    │
│ 1842.                                                                 │
└─────────────────────────────────────────────────────────────────────┘
```

hyperlinks in both alphabetical and chronological order. Be sure to check out the History Topics Index, which links to a series of articles on the development of mathematical ideas such as "Pi Through the Ages" and "Babylonian and Egyptian Mathematics."

INTEGRATION IDEAS

• Math and gender
Ask students if they noticed that most of the mathematicians throughout history were white males. Why might this be? Discuss the social, cultural, and historical factors that shaped math history—for example, women generally weren't permitted to attend universities in the 1800s.

• Multicultural
As they browse the site, have students keep a journal of mathematical discoveries made by non-Europeans.

OTHER SITES RELATED TO THIS TOPIC

Database of Student Research in Math
   URL: gopher://hub.terc.edu:70/11/hub/math
MathSource Gopher
   URL: gopher://gopher.wri.com
Math Articles, Papers, Reports, and Newsletters
   URL: gopher://hub.terc.edu:70/11/hub/math

MATH MAGIC PROJECT

URL: http://forum.swarthmore.edu/mathmagic

MathMagic is a K-12 telecommunications project that provides strong motivation for students to use computer technology while increasing problem-solving strategies and communications skills. MathMagic posts challenges in each of four categories (K-3, 4-6, 7-9, and 10-12). Registered teams of students work together to solve them. One solution is posted for every pair. MathMagic is widely accepted by hundreds of online users because it addresses most of the standards of the National Council of Teachers of Mathematics.

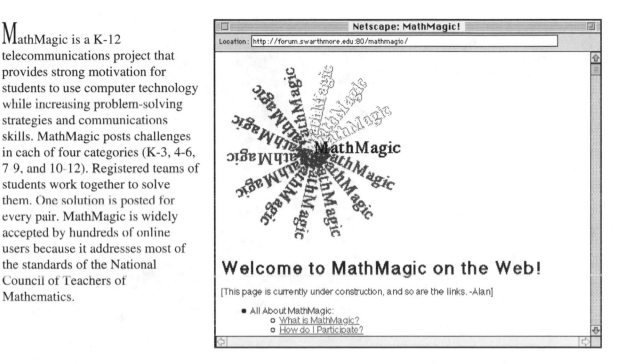

INTEGRATION IDEAS

• Math home pages
Since teams may put home pages on the Web, have your student teams design their own math home pages. Explore the pages of other teams first.

• Math challenge
Access problems posted by project coordinators at the following address. Look for the subdirectory that corresponds with your grade level.
URL: ftp://forum.swarthmore.edu/mathmagic/

OTHER SITES RELATED TO THIS TOPIC

Digital Resource Center for Mathematics
    URL: http://e-math.ams.org/web/
Math Software for Students
    URL: http://gams.nist.gov

MEGAMATH

URL: http://www.c3.lanl.gov/mega-math/

The language at this Web site says it best: "Mathematics is a live science—new discoveries are made every day. The frontier of mathematics is an exciting place where mathematicians experiment and play with creative and imaginative ideas. Some of these ideas are readily accessible to students, but other concepts (infinity is a good example) that pique childrens' curiosity are not widely understood or available. The MegaMath project brings some of those unusual or important mathematical ideas to elementary school classrooms so young people and their teachers can think about them together."

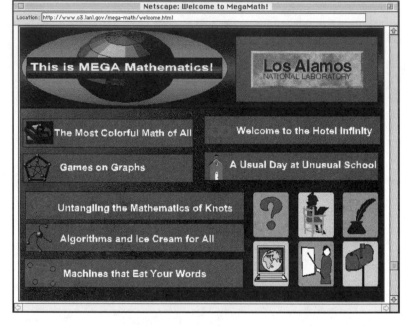

INTEGRATION IDEAS

• Teacher tips
Each of the seven activities has an Activities and an Evaluation page. Use these links to find ideas for integrating each activity into your classroom.

• Teachers talk
Another section of the site contains more than a dozen writings by classroom teachers about how they integrated MegaMath into their curriculum. **URL: http://www.c3.lanl.gov/mega-math/write.html**

OTHER SITES RELATED TO THIS TOPIC

General Math Resources
> **URL: gopher://okinawa.wri.com**
> **URL: news:k12.ed.math**
> **URL: news:sci.math**

Internet Resources for Mathematics Educators Database
> **URL: gopher://gopher.nwrel.org:70/11/programs/same/**

W E B C A L C

URL: http://www.charm.net/~web/Calc.html

A very useful, fun implementation of current World Wide Web technology is WebCalc, the world's first completely online calculator. All of the functions are here, from addition to division. Though this Web site is surely not going to replace that plain vanilla calculator in your desk drawer, it is an interesting Web tool meant to be used by teachers and students.

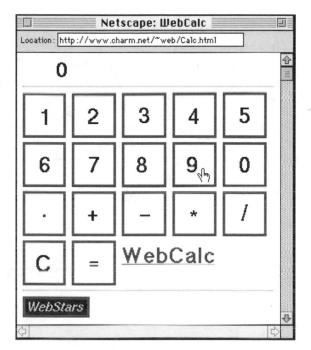

INTEGRATION IDEAS

• Test drive
Have students try the online calculator. Have them compare it to regular calculators. How could it be improved? Made to run faster? Is this good use of the technology?

• Be an inventor
After trying this calculator, have students think of other common devices that could be put onto the Web. How would they work?

OTHER SITES RELATED TO THIS TOPIC

High School Math & Science Pages
        URL: http://euclid.math.fsu.edu/Science/highsch.html
Online Calculator II
        URL: http://guinan.gsfc.nasa.gov/Web/Calc.html
Virtual Library of Mathematics
        URL: http://euclid.math.fsu.edu/Science/math.html

WORLD WIDE WEB VIRTUAL LIBRARY: MATHEMATICS

URL: http://euclid.math.fsu.edu/Science/math.html

The math index located at the World Wide Web Virtual Library will make a great home page for math wizards and neophytes. The site's links to online resources for math teachers and students are organized by categories such as Mathematical Software, Electronic Journals, and Specialized Fields. Click on the General Resources icon, for example, and you'll travel to a huge page of math hyperlinks, ranging from the American Mathematical Society to Technical Math Books.

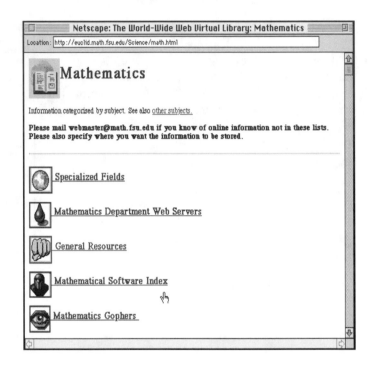

INTEGRATION IDEA

● **Research tool**

In preparation for an upcoming research paper or project, have your math, algebra, geometry, or calculus students look up possible online sources of information on the subject using this Web index.

OTHER SITES RELATED TO THIS TOPIC

Math Resources at Carrie's Crazy Quilt for Educators
    URL: http://www.mtjeff.com:80/~bodenst/page5.html#math
Georgia State University Mathematics & Computer Science Department
    URL: http://www.cs.gsu.edu/math/othermath.html
Catalog of Mathematics Resources on the Internet
    URL: http://mthwww.uwc.edu/wwwmahes/files/math01.htm

CHAPTER

SCIENCE

ANATOMY IMAGE BROWSER

URL: http://www.vis.colostate.edu/cgi-bin/gva/gvaview

The Anatomy Web Browser will excite students about anatomy. This site provides a fun, interactive way to view computer-generated images and movies of internal organs and bones—all online. The home page has a list of more than 30 animation sequences that students can call up and manipulate. Sequences include All bones and cartilage, All bones without cartilage, Spine with cartilage, Ribs only, Just the skin, Bones and tissue, Heart, arteries, and veins, Lungs and bronchi, and more.

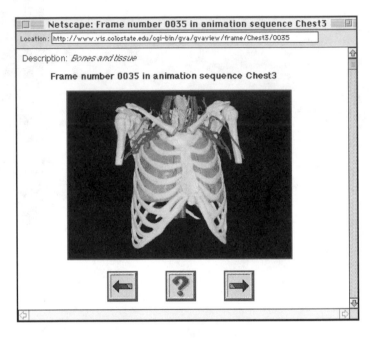

INTEGRATION IDEAS

• Journal
Assign groups of students different sections and functions of the body to explore via this site. Have them keep a journal and report on their activities and findings or include the information in a paper or project.

• Teaching tool
Gather your class wherever your school has Net access. Use this site to manipulate the images as you discuss each body part or organ.

OTHER SITES RELATED TO THIS TOPIC

Heart Anatomy Tour
URL: http://lenti.med.umn.edu/anatomy/heartblo.html
The Whole Brain Atlas
URL: http://www.med.harvard.edu/AANLIB/home.html
Visible Human Anatomy Project
URL: http://www.nlm.nih.gov/extramural_research.dir/visible_human.html

APOLLO 11 MISSION TO THE MOON

URL: http://www.gsfc.nasa.gov/hqpao/apollo_11.html

Sponsored by NASA, the Apollo 11 Mission to the Moon Web site is a valuable resource about this historic space mission. Relive Apollo 11's historic flight as you read recollections of the astronauts, key White House documents, a retrospective analysis, and a bibliography. You can also view short video clips of the most exciting moments of the mission and download a 25th anniversary poster (suitable for color printing) or a mission patch. Students can even learn about NASA's rich history, from its beginnings in 1915 as the National Advisory Committee for Aeronautics to the full-fledged agency it is today.

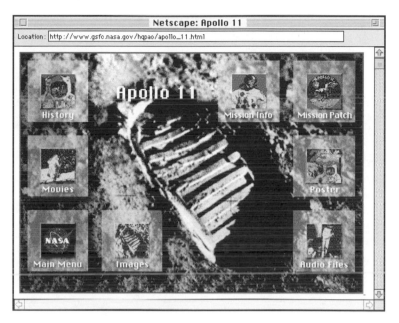

INTEGRATION IDEAS

• Timeline
Using information on the site and in the library, have students create a colorful timeline highlighting at least five of NASA's most historic space missions.

• Interviews
After accessing this site, ask students to interview parents and others about their recollections of the Apollo missions and where they were when the first man walked on the moon.

OTHER SITES RELATED TO THIS TOPIC

Apollo Missions
        URL: http://www.ksc.nasa.gov/history/apollo/apollo.html
        URL: http://images.jsc.nasa.gov/html/apollo.htm
Astronomy Newsgroups
        URL: news:sci.aeronautics
        URL: news:sci.astro.hubble

BIODIVERSITY AND BIOLOGICAL COLLECTIONS

URL: http://muse.bio.cornell.edu

Within the pages of this site you will find information about specimens in biological collections, taxonomic authority files, directories of biologists, archives of the Taxacom and MUSE-L online mailing lists, access to online biological journals (including Flora On-line) and information about biodiversity projects worldwide. Recently added are index images to the Biological Image Archive, a large collection of animal and plant images stored at Cornell University. A must visit for all high school and college biology students.

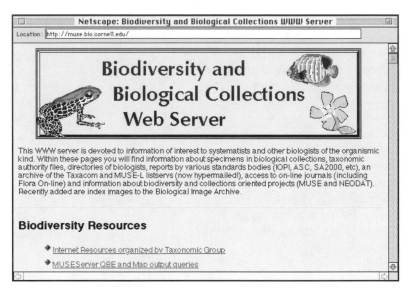

Netscape: Biodiversity and Biological Collections WWW Server

Location: http://muse.bio.cornell.edu/

Biodiversity and Biological Collections Web Server

This WWW server is devoted to information of interest to systematists and other biologists of the organismic kind. Within these pages you will find information about specimens in biological collections, taxonomic authority files, directories of biologists, reports by various standards bodies (IOPI, ASC, SA2000, etc), an archive of the Taxacom and MUSE-L listservs (now hypermailed!), access to on-line journals (including Flora On-line) and information about biodiversity and collections oriented projects (MUSE and NEODAT). Recently added are index images to the Biological Image Archive.

Biodiversity Resources

♦ Internet Resources organized by Taxonomic Group

♦ MUSE Server QBE and Map output queries

INTEGRATION IDEA

• Mailing lists

Expose students to the various online mailing list archives to show them how biology is a changing science. Allow them time to review recent postings to the lists to see what topics are being discussed. Then, have them sign up and ask questions of the experts online. Be sure they keep a journal of the posts they've sent and received. This could be a three- to nine-month project.

OTHER SITES RELATED TO THIS TOPIC

Natural History Museums and Biological Collections
   URL: http://muse.bio.cornell.edu/museums/
Mammalogy Resources
   URL: http://muse.bio.cornell.edu/taxonomy/mammal.html
Botany Resources
   URL: http://muse.bio.cornell.edu/taxonomy/botany.html

DNA TO DINOSAURS

URL: http://www.bvis.uic.edu/museum/exhibits/Exhibits.html

Children can't get enough of dinosaurs. So here's a fun, educational Web site about dinosaurs that's ideal for students in all grade levels. They can view pictures of more than two dozen different dinosaurs. Students can watch online video clips of an Albertosaurus, Apatosaurus, and Triceratops going about their daily business and listen to the 100 million year forecast for the Triassic Period—even look at a 3D image of a Tyrannosaurus Rex tooth!

INTEGRATION IDEAS

• Research
Have students write a research paper about their favorite dinosaur and use information and images retrieved from this site to make a "Day in the Life" story.

• Teacher aids
Go to the following location for an in-depth teacher's guide to integrating materials into your existing curriculum.
URL: http://www.bvis.uic.edu/museum/education/LOTguide1.html

OTHER SITES RELATED TO THIS TOPIC

Dinosaur Exhibits
      URL: http://www.hcc.hawaii.edu/dinos/dinos.1.html
      URL: http://ucmp1.berkeley.edu/exhibittext/cladecham.html
Dinosaur Tongue Twisters (English)
      URL: http://www.bvis.uic.edu/museum/Media_page.html

EARTH VIEWER

URL: http://www.fourmilab.ch/earthview/vplanet.html

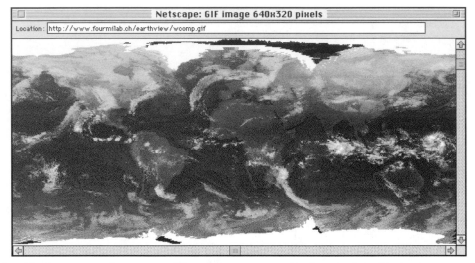

Students can look down at the Earth as if they were in space via this site. They can view a map of the Earth showing the day and night regions at the current moment. Or, they can look at the Earth from the Sun, the Moon, the night side of the Earth, above any location on the planet specified by latitude, longitude and altitude, or from a satellite in Earth orbit. Images can be generated based on a topographical map of the Earth, up-to-date weather satellite imagery, or a composite image of cloud cover superimposed on a map of the Earth.

INTEGRATION IDEAS

• Time zones
Students can use images at this site to write and illustrate a report about why time zones and the International Date Line were created.

• Writing project
After younger students visit the site, have them choose a location on the globe and write a story about what children in that country would be doing at the same "time" as they're getting out of bed, going to school, or sleeping at night.

OTHER SITES RELATED TO THIS TOPIC

Astronomy Gopher & Ftp Sites
   URL: gopher://gopher.gsfc.nasa.gov
   URL: ftp://huntress.jpl.nasa.gov
   URL: ftp://explorer.arc.nasa.gov/pub/SPACE
Astronomy Software
   URL: http://www.fourmilab.ch:80/homeplanet/

ENTOMOLOGY AT COLORADO STATE

URL: http://www.ColoState.edu/Depts/Entomology/ent.html

Students and teachers who love to "bug out" will appreciate this Web site—it's got links to just about every entomology-related resource on the Internet. You'll find entries for insect photos and drawings, MPEG and QuickTime movies, related newsletters and journals, and other university entomology departments and organizations. It also features entomology gopher sites, newsgroups, mailing lists, and BBSs; entomology degree programs around the world; and even employment opportunities. Browse these pages to get an idea of the incredible diversity of insect species and the scientific disciplines that study them.

Netscape: GIF image 640x480 pixels
Location: http://www.colostate.edu/Depts/Entomology/images/kbees.gif

INTEGRATION IDEAS

• Lady beetles
Use this site to link your class to the Lady Beetle Survey in Canada, an ongoing project conducted to save native species from dangerous, exotic species.

• Local bugs
Have students use this site to research insect species in their community and create a report. Have them try to find if recent discoveries have created new knowledge about the species.

OTHER SITES RELATED TO THIS TOPIC

Biology - The Tree of Life
   URL: http://phylogeny.arizona.edu/tree/phylogeny.html
Education Programs for Professional Entomology (Vocational Education)
   URL: http://www.ColoState.edu/Depts/Entomology/ent.html

THE FRANKLIN INSTITUTE SCIENCE MUSEUM

URL: http://sln.fi.edu

Begin your visit to this nationally-acclaimed science museum by touring more than two dozen online exhibits, including the Glimpses of Benjamin Franklin exhibit and The Heart: A Virtual Exploration. The Institutes' educational hotlists point to educational hotspots on the Internet. If you're interested in the continually changing world of current science, visit the

vast publications library, where you'll find science news, activities, and resources. Consider using one of the online units of study to support your science curriculum.
URL:http://sln.fi.edu/tfi/video/welcome.mov

INTEGRATION IDEAS

• Ben Franklin
Benjamin Franklin was truly a Renaissance man. Have students use this site to learn about Franklin the scientist. Make sure they sample the sound and video clips recreating some of his accomplishments. What would he have thought of the Internet? How would he have used it?

• Teacher aids
Several online units of study are available to integrate this site into your existing science curriculum.
URL: http://sln.fi.edu/tfi/units/units.html

OTHER SITES RELATED TO THIS TOPIC

Philadelphia Inquirer Online (English/Literature)
    URL: http://sln.fi.edu/tfi/publications/inquirer/inq.html
History of Computers (History)
    URL: http://calypso.cs.uregina.ca/Lecture/

HANDS ON CHILDREN'S MUSEUM

URL: http://www.wln.com/~deltapac/hocm.html

Billed as "a fun place to be for kids 10 years old and under," the Hands On Children's Museum Web site is a colorful, fun place for young students to learn about science. All of the museum's current online exhibits are ocean related. The main exhibit is called Ocean Odyssey and links students to online pictures of marine mammals, sea birds, and interactive ocean exhibits on other Internet computers. To get directly to the Ocean Odyssey exhibit, enter the following address into your Web browser.

URL: http://www.wln.com/~deltapac/ocean_od.html

INTEGRATION IDEA

● Teacher aids
Several lesson plans and student activities concerning whales and other marine mammals can be found at the following related Internet sites.
URL: http://www.bev.net/education/SeaWorld/teacherguides.html
URL: http://curry.edschool.Virginia.EDU/~kpj5e/Whales/Contents.HTML
URL: http://curry.edschool.Virginia.EDU/~kpj5e/Whales/Research.HTML
URL: http://curry.edschool.Virginia.EDU/~kpj5e/Whales/Poem.HTML

OTHER SITES RELATED TO THIS TOPIC

Wondering About Whales Unit (English/Literature)
    URL: http://curry.edschool.Virginia.EDU/~kpj5e/Whales/WonAbout.HTML
History of Whaling Unit (History)
    URL: http://curry.edschool.Virginia.EDU/~kpj5e/Whales/HisWhaling.HTML
Whales: A Thematic Math Unit (Mathematics)
    URL: http://curry.edschool.Virginia.EDU/~kpj5e/Whales/StuMath.HTML

SCIENCE BYTES

URL: http://loki.ur.utk.edu/ut2kids/science.html

Science Bytes is designed for elementary and secondary school students and teachers. Each installment describes the work done by scientists at the University of Tennessee. The organizers hope to educate Internauts about current science questions and issues and inspire you to pursue new questions and exciting projects in the classroom. A recent issue contained interactive articles about marmosets, dragonflies,

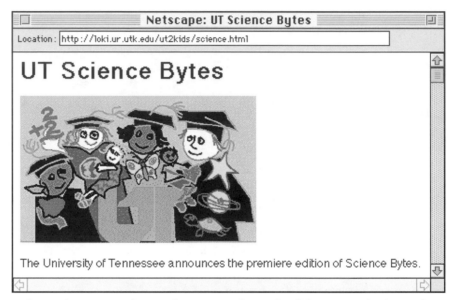

forensic anthropologists, information on how mapmakers make maps, and a study of the seasons in Antarctica.

INTEGRATION IDEAS

• Antarctic search
Have younger students visit the site's Search for Antarctic Spring story. It tracks the experiences of a college student aboard the Polar Duke as it engages in scientific discovery.

• Discussion
Break students into groups and have each choose an article from the current issue for study and discussion.

OTHER SITES RELATED TO THIS TOPIC

Digital Science Theater
URL: http://www.ncsa.uiuc.edu/SDG/DigitalGallery/DG_science_theater.html
Resource Guides to Science
URL: gopher://una.hh.lib.umich.edu:70/11/inetdirsstacks
Science Articles
URL: gopher://gopher.well.sf.ca.us:70/11/Science

VIRTUAL FROG DISSECTION KIT

URL: http://george.lbl.gov/ITG.hm.pg.docs/dissect/info.html

Designed for high school biology classes, this Web site allows students to explore the anatomy of a frog without dissecting a real animal. They can turn the frog over, remove its skin and selected organs, even view online movies of the frog rotating in various directions for a better view! A tutorial for using the Dissection Kit can be found here.
URL: http://www-itg.lbl.gov/vfrog/tutorial/tutorial contents.html

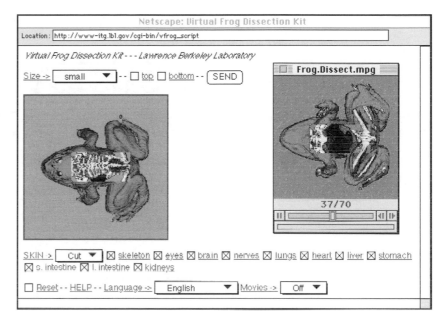

INTEGRATION IDEAS

• Foreign language
Use the site's ability to function in more than eight languages. Integrate biology and foreign language studies by having students dissect the frog via another language. **URL: http://george.lbl.gov/ITG.hm.pg.docs/dissect/translations.html**

• Compare and contrast
If your class dissects a real frog, have your students logon to the site after they've completed their "real" dissection. Have them compare the real versus the online experience. Which did they prefer? Why?

OTHER SITES RELATED TO THIS TOPIC

NetFrog Dissection
    URL: http://curry.edschool.Virginia.EDU:80/~insttech/frog/
Virtual Frog Builder Game
    URL: http://www-itg.lbl.gov/vfrog/builder.info.html
Virtual Tick Dissection
    URL: http://www.public.iastate.edu/~entomology/Images/TickDissection/EntireSequence.html

VOLCANOWORLD

URL: http://volcano.und.nodak.edu/

Volcanoes are one of the most dramatic phenomena in nature, attracting millions of visitors each year to national parks and fascinating millions of children in school science courses. VolcanoWorld, maintained by NASA, can greatly enrich the learning experience by delivering high quality images and interactive experiments that add depth, variety and currency to existing volcano information sources. VolcanoWorld has a very easy-to-use, hypercard-like interface which has links to updates on current volcanic activity, information on how volcanoes work

and how to become a volcanologist, historical eruptions, and online forms you can use to sign your class up for the ongoing Ask a Volcanologist Project. The site includes several lesson plan ideas centering on volcanoes.
URL: http://volcano.und.nodak.edu/vwdocs/vwlessons/vwlesson.html

INTEGRATION IDEA

• Adopt a volcano

After your students spend some time at this site, have them each "adopt" a volcano for the duration of the school year. Have them use current volcano information from the site to track the activity of their volcano. They could graph or chart the results and ask a volcanologist to interpret them.

OTHER SITES RELATED TO THIS TOPIC

Volcanoes & Volcanology
  URL: http://vulcan.wr.usgs.gov
  URL: http://www.geo.mtu.edu/eos/
  URL: http://www.yahoo.com/Science/Geology_and_Geophysics/Volcanoes/
Volcanoes (Art)
  URL: http://volcano.und.nodak.edu/vwdocs/vw_hyperexchange/art.html

WEB ELEMENTS

URL: http://www-c8.lanl.gov/infosys/html/periodic/periodic-main.html

Welcome to the Internet's definitive online Periodic Table of the Elements. Each element on the chart can be clicked to discover its full name, atomic number, atomic symbol, atomic weight, electron configuration, and its history. Another version of this site can be found here. **URL: http://www.cchem.berkeley.edu/Table/index.html**

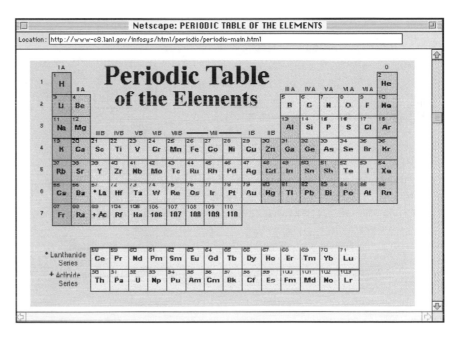

INTEGRATION IDEAS

• Demonstration

Use this online Table of the Elements to show your students the power of the Web and its ability to link related information together.

• Research project

Have your students pick an element from the table to research, and require them to use the site as a research source. The following site is also helpful. **URL: gopher://ucsbuxa.ucsb.edu:3001/11/.Sciences/.Chemistry/**

OTHER SITES RELATED TO THIS TOPIC

Chemistry Resources via Gopher
> **URL: gopher://marvel.loc.gov/11/global/sci/chem**

Periodic Table of the Elements via Gopher
> **URL: gopher://ucsbuxa.ucsb.edu:3001/11/.Sciences/.Chemistry/.periodic.table**

WELCOME TO THE NANOWORLD

URL: http://www.uq.oz.au/nanoworld/nanohome.html

The Nanoworld, defined as "a place which is only accessible with powerful electron microscopes," is now visible to Internauts via this fantastic Web site provided by the University of Queensland in Australia. The Images Gallery will let you view ants, blood cells, parasitic worm eggs, and rat hairs (yuck!) magnified thousands of times by electron microscopes, light microscopes, and x-ray diffraction equipment. Some of the images are large and may take a while to load to your computer, but they're well worth the wait.

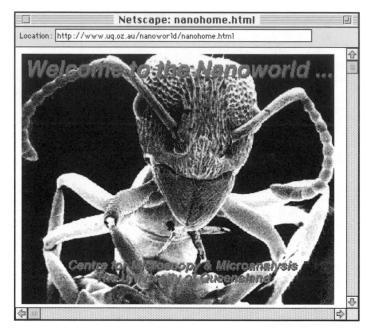

INTEGRATION IDEAS

• Compare and contrast
Instruct students to use links at the site to explore the concepts of scale and magnification and compare some familiar objects.

• Art work
For some creative fun time, have students pick an object, such as a fingernail, and sketch how they think it might look like using an electron microscope. Then, have them visit the site to see how it really appears.

OTHER SITES RELATED TO THIS TOPIC

Microscopes and Microscopy
   URL: http://metro.turnpike.net/jefferie/index.html
Entomology
   URL: http://www.uq.oz.au/entomology/home.html
Digitized Electron Micrographs of Viruses
   URL: http://www.bocklabs.wisc.edu/em.html

YAHOO'S INDEX OF SCIENCE RESOURCES

URL: http://www.yahoo.com/Science/

This Web page lists more than 5,000 links to science-related material on the Internet. The list of topics indexed includes Acoustics, Agriculture, Artificial Life, Chaos, Ecology, Energy, Genealogy, Magazines, Meteorology, Museums, Oceanography, Physics, Space, and Zoology. If it's on the Internet and has something to do with science, chances are a pointer to it can be found here.

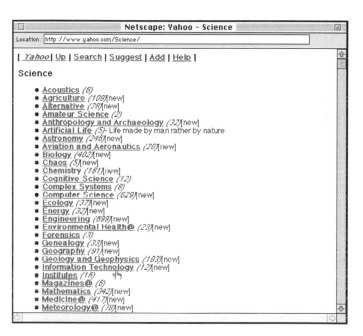

INTEGRATION IDEA

• Research

In preparation for an upcoming research paper or project, have your science students look up possible online sources of information about the topic using this online index.

OTHER SITES RELATED TO THIS TOPIC

Galaxy's Internet Science Resources Index
> **URL: http://galaxy.einet.net/galaxy/Science.html**

Science Newsgroups
> **URL: news:k12.ed.science**   **URL: news:sci.answers**
> **URL: news:sci.anthropology**   **URL: news:sci.bio.conservation**

CHAPTER

SOCIAL SCIENCES/
HUMANITIES

131

A R C T I C   C I R C L E

URL: http://www.lib.uconn.edu/ArcticCircle/

The highly informative Arctic Circle site is a find for students of sociology, culture, anthropology, and environmental issues. The designers present three themes they feel are "crucial to the future of the people, land, and waters of the Arctic and Subarctic region: natural resources; culture and social equity; and environmental justice." You'll find hyperlinked articles such as "Sustainability, Equity, and Environmental Protection," photographs of the region, and audio and video clips. Most of the material in this multimedia presentation is adapted from publications by Norman Chance, a prominent cultural and environmental anthropologist and author involved in several long-term research projects in the Arctic region.

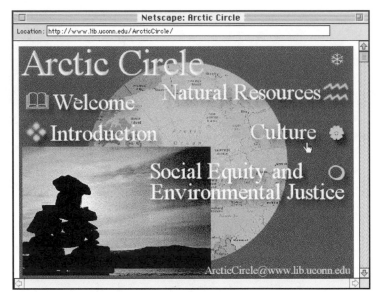

INTEGRATION IDEAS

• Misconceptions
Before they visit the site, have students list what they know about the Arctic environment, Eskimos and Native American peoples, and the geography and land uses of northern regions. Have them use the site to discover any misconceptions they may have.

• Development issues
Discuss the problematic issue of economic and social development versus the rights of indigenous peoples. Compare what's happening in the Arctic with events in the rain forests of South America.

OTHER SITES RELATED TO THIS TOPIC

Arctic Centre - University of Lapland
>   URL: http://www.urova.fi/arktinen/index.html

Northern Explorer
>   URL: http://www.finite-tech.com

The Alaskan Center
>   URL: http://www.alaskan.com

CHRISTIAN CLASSICS ETHEREAL LIBRARY

URL: http://www.cs.pitt.edu:80/~planting/books

Students of classic religious and theological texts will want to visit this virtual library, the online home of great Christian works such as Bunyan's *Pilgrim's Progress* and *The Confessions of St. Augustine,* and *The Imitation of Christ* by Thomas à Kempis. Among the public domain works here you'll also find classics from Calvin, Donne, Milton, and many more. Texts are available in numerous formats, including plain text, Postscript, Adobe PDF, and Hypercard, but the online Web versions make for easy reading and navigation. To quote a line from the home page, "There is enough good reading material here to last you a lifetime, if you give each work the time it deserves!"

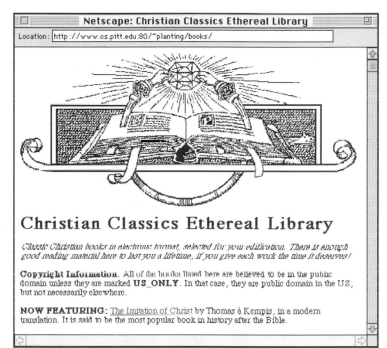

Netscape: Christian Classics Ethereal Library

Location: http://www.cs.pitt.edu:80/~planting/books/

Christian Classics Ethereal Library

Classic Christian books in electronic format, selected for your edification. There is enough good reading material here to last you a lifetime, if you give each work the time it deserves!

Copyright Information. All of the books listed here are believed to be in the public domain unless they are marked **US_ONLY**. In that case, they are public domain in the US, but not necessarily elsewhere.

NOW FEATURING: The Imitation of Christ by Thomas à Kempis, in a modern translation. It is said to be the most popular book in history after the Bible.

INTEGRATION IDEA

• Electronic books

Research how these books were originally published. Discuss the differences between how they were distributed in the authors' days versus the electronic dissemination of books today. What are the advantages and disadvantages? How might the format of a work affect its tone? What is lost with these electronic translations? What is gained?

OTHER SITES RELATED TO THIS TOPIC

Matthew Henry's Concise Commentary on the Whole Bible
URL: http://www.cs.pitt.edu/~planting/books/henry/mhc/mhc.html
Bible Gateway
URL: http://www.calvin.edu/cgi-bin/bible
Religious Articles and Books
URL: gopher://wiretap.spies.com:70/11/Library

DEAD SEA SCROLLS EXHIBIT

URL:http://sunsite.unc.edu/expo/deadsea.scrolls.exhibit/intro.html

This online version of the "Scrolls from the Dead Sea: The Ancient Library of Qumran and Modern Scholarship" exhibit at the Library of Congress allows future archaeologists to examine the famous scrolls without taking a field trip to Washington, D.C. The exhibition "covers the Jewish and Christian context of the scrolls and the Qumran community that deposited them, and includes images not only of selected pieces of the scrolls, but of other archaeological artifacts, such as pottery and coins." The site contains a wealth of information, but sifting through it still doesn't take as long as a real dig!

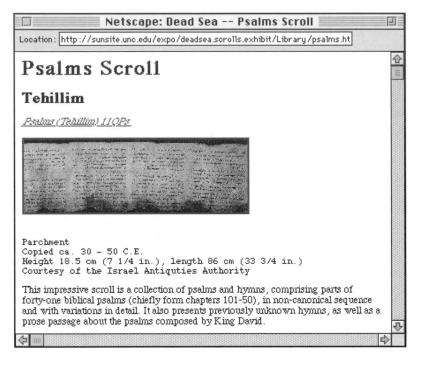

Netscape: Dead Sea -- Psalms Scroll

Location: http://sunsite.unc.edu/expo/deadsea.scrolls.exhibit/Library/psalms.ht

Psalms Scroll

Tehillim

Psalms (Tehillim) 11QPs

Parchment
Copied ca. 30 – 50 C.E.
Height 18.5 cm (7 1/4 in.), length 86 cm (33 3/4 in.)
Courtesy of the Israel Antiquties Authority

This impressive scroll is a collection of psalms and hymns, comprising parts of forty-one biblical psalms (chiefly form chapters 101-50), in non-canonical sequence and with variations in detail. It also presents previously unknown hymns, as well as a prose passage about the psalms composed by King David.

INTEGRATION IDEA

• Artifact access

After students tour the site, start a class discussion on the issue of intellectual freedom and the right to "scholarly access" of artifacts such as the scrolls and the Shroud of Turin. Should such finds be immediately open to a wide audience? Under what circumstances could researchers seal access to artifacts? Who owns ancient items and should they be sold?

OTHER SITES RELATED TO THIS TOPIC

Archaeology newsgroups
> **URL: news:sci.archaeology**
> **URL: news:sci.classics**

Classics and Mediterranean Archaeology
> **URL: http://rome.classics.lsa.umich.edu/welcome.html**

DEMOGRAPHY AND POPULATION STUDIES

URL: http://coombs.anu.edu.au/ResFacilities/DemographyPage.html

This site certainly qualifies as the one-stop shopping place for demography information. Students can explore numerous societal forces to find out how immigration and population migration affects the environment and economy, what happens when population levels and birth or death rates change, and what

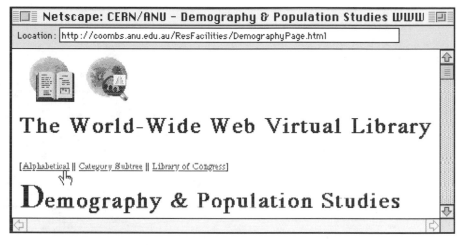

consequences shifting marriage patterns might have. Numerous databases are available, including ones from the U.S. Census Bureau, International Institute for Sustainable Development, Office of Social and Economic Data, and the World Health Organization. No fancy graphics here (dig around a little and you'll find some decent charts and graphs), but these pages are loaded with information and links to data galore.

INTEGRATION IDEAS

• Demographers
Start a class discussion on the growing importance of professional demographers. Why is it critical to recognize trends concerning population growth, natural resource consumption, and environmental damage? What trends did students discover that affect their local area?

• Data comparison
Have students graph census data and look for patterns and regional trends for their area.

OTHER SITES RELATED TO THIS TOPIC

Environmental Protection Agency's Future Studies Gopher
URL: gopher://futures.wic.epa.gov
Project GeoSim Interactive Information Server
URL: http://geosim.cs.vt.edu
U.S. State Department Background Notes
URL: gopher://umslvma.umsl.edu:70/11/LIBRARY/GOVDOCS/BNOTES

ELECTRONIC NEWSSTAND

URL: http://www.enews.com

The Electronic Newsstand, long one of the Internet's most popular sites, is known for its up-to-date database of current news from dozens of the world's most popular magazines. Now, the Newsstand has graduated to the World Wide Web, and its slick graphical interface makes it easier than ever to find the current information students are looking for. Here's just a sampling of the magazines, newspapers, and other online news services represented in its data files: *Business Week, Discover, St. Petersburg Times, TimesLink* from the *Los Angeles Times, The Internet Letter, HeadsUp* personal daily news service, *EnviroKnow* for environmental professionals, *Tribune Internet Newspaper, The Village Voice,* and *Classroom Connect.*

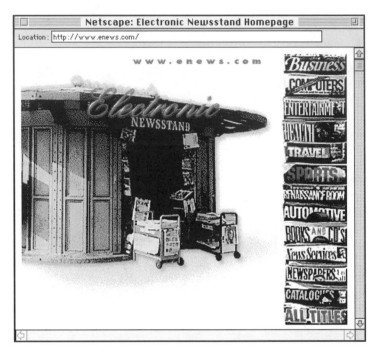

INTEGRATION IDEAS

• News online
Have students browse the publications. How do online publications differ from traditional ones? What are their strengths and weaknesses? Have them design an online publication of their own.

• Keyword search
Assign students topics to search for via the keyword search feature of this site and report on what they find.

OTHER SITES RELATED TO THIS TOPIC

DowVision & Wall Street Journal Business News
URL: http://dowvision.wais.net
General Internet News
URL: news:comp.internet.net-happenings
InfoSeek Computer Publications Archives
URL: http://www.infoseek.com

EVERTON GENEALOGY PAGE

URL: http://www.xmission.com/~jayhall/

The extensive Everton Genealogy Page is perfect for those new to the topic and for experienced ancestry researchers. The first link, Getting Started with your Genealogy, provides basic, practical pointers on beginning a search for family roots and putting together family trees.

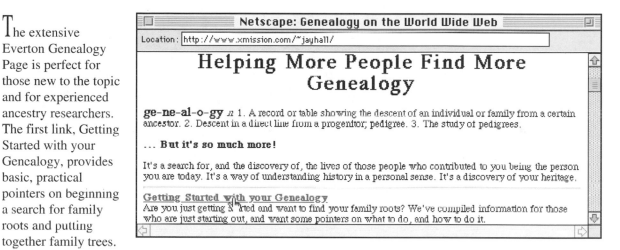

The Links to Library Resources area will take you to hundreds of catalogs and exhibits useful for tracing lineage and finding information about family origins. Best of all, you'll find links to just about every genealogy resource on the Internet, including other Web pages such as the National Archives of the United States, mailing lists, newsgroups, and ftp sites.

INTEGRATION IDEA

• Family history

Arrange an online session after school involving students and their parents and/or grandparents. Prepare students by accessing the research outline. Allow each family group to explore the resources on the Internet to find information related to their specific history.

OTHER SITES RELATED TO THIS TOPIC

Adoptee Page from Carrie's Crazy Quilt
      URL: http://www.mtjeff.com/~bodenst/page3.html
Genealogy Home Page
      URL: http://ftp.cac.psu.edu:80/~saw/genealogy.html
Genealogy newsgroups
      URL: news:soc.genealogy

F E D W O R L D

URL: http://www.fedworld.gov

The National Technical Information Service (NTIS) introduced FedWorld in November 1992 to meet the challenge of putting U.S. government information online. In an electronic age when more government agencies are racing to get online, the goal of NTIS FedWorld is to provide a one-stop location for people to locate, order, and find U.S. government information. FedWorld can be accessed using the Internet telnet or Web command at **fedworld.gov** and provides access to more than 130 government bulletin boards and databases.

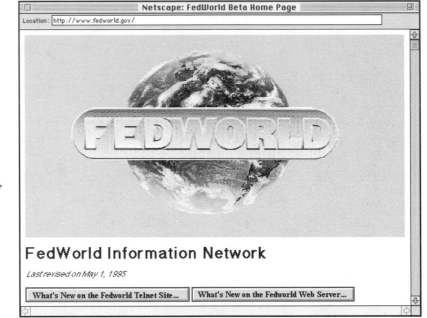

INTEGRATION IDEAS

• The Thirties

Have students visit the following "Voice of the Thirties" location to read excerpts of interviews with people of the time. Compare home and work life of those times with that of today. **URL: http://lcweb2.loc.gov/wpaintro/exhome.html**

• Government online

Have students access at least five government databases and report on their value to citizens. Will the existence of government information online affect democracy?

OTHER SITES RELATED TO THIS TOPIC

Recent U.S. Government Reports
    URL: http://www.fedworld.gov/preview/preview.html
U.S. Electronic Open Meetings
    URL: http://meeting.fedworld.gov/

GLOBAL NETWORK NAVIGATOR INDEX

URL: http://gnn.com/gnn/wic/index.html

This comprehensive Internet information center, maintained by O'Reilly and Associates (producer of NCSA Mosaic), is an excellent starting point for teachers and students looking for social science and/or humanities resources. Select the Whole Internet Catalog button, wait for the index to download, and scroll down to find Humanities and Social Science links. They'll take you to hundreds of sites with material on anthropology, archaeology, politics, Black and African studies, women's studies, philosophy, law, and much more.

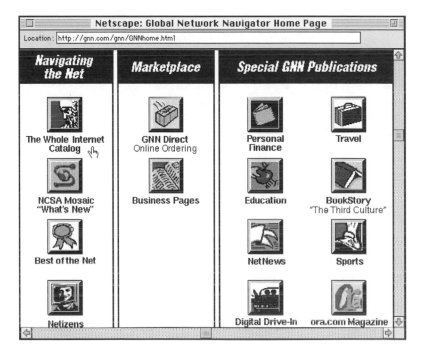

INTEGRATION IDEA

● **General research**

In preparation for an upcoming research paper or project, have your social science or humanities students look up possible online sources of information on the subject using this Web index.

OTHER SITES RELATED TO THIS TOPIC

Social Science & Humanities Indexes at Yahoo
  URL: http://www.yahoo.com/Social_Science/
  URL: http://www.yahoo.com/Society_and_Culture/
Social Science Index at EINet Galaxy
  URL: http://galaxy.einet.net/galaxy/Social-Sciences.html

INTERNET PUBLIC LIBRARY

URL: http://ipl.sils.umich.edu

The Internet Public Library is an experimental project that, for the first time, blends the traditions and culture of libraries with the dynamic world of the Internet. Here you'll find an exhibit hall with links to the latest online cultural showcases, an online classroom where educators and other specialists hold classes, a youth division that features original stories from children, professional resources for librarians, and much more. Says the Director: "We are not attempting simply to put in a public library up on the Internet or mindlessly translate the functions of libraries to the Net environment. We are also not trying to replace existing libraries or supplant the valuable services they provide to their communities. Rather, we hope to complement their work in appropriate ways." Be sure to check out the Youth Division's wonderfully interactive features that include online illustrated

(some include audio!) storybooks, story and Internet contests, book reviews by kids, an ask the author section, and more. **URL: http://ipl.sils.umich.edu/youth/HomePage2.html**

INTEGRATION IDEAS

• Read a story
Young students can visit Story Hour and page through books such as *Do Spiders Live on the World Wide Web?* This simple, whimsical story is a great way to teach young children computer and Net terms.

• Get interactive
Have students submit stories, book reviews, or questions to authors via this site to understand the Internet's interactivity.

OTHER SITES RELATED TO THIS TOPIC

CARL Gateway to Library Networks
> **URL: telnet://pac.carl.org**

Innovative Internet Applications in Libraries Database
> **URL: http://frank.mtsu.edu/~kmiddlet/libweb/innovate.html**

Online Libraries via Yahoo
> **URL: http://ww.yahoo.com/Reference/Libraies**

ISLAND NATIONS OF POLYNESIA

URL: http://mana.byuh.edu/docs/Culture.htm

Here is the complete guide to the Polynesian culture, from arts, crafts, and music to an in-depth exploration of the government and languages. This is a colorful, rich site full of interesting information. Students can access the site's language-related resources to add to their understanding of the inhabitants' native tongues.
URL: http://www.olelo.hawaii.edu
The site also contains an incredible wealth of cultural information about the people of the Polynesian Nations.
URL: http://mana.byuh.edu/docs/People.htm

Netscape: Culture.htm

Location: http://mana.byuh.edu/docs/Culture.htm

An In-Depth Look at the Island Nations of Polynesia:

Agriculture | Arts & Crafts | Canoes | Communications | Economy | Education | Food (recipes) | Genealogy | General | Geography | Government | Health & Medicine | History | Languages | Legends | Leisure (games) | Literature | Maps | Music & Dance | People | Philosophy | Plants | Science | Tourism | Values & Traditions

Demographic Information from World Atlas by Mindscape 415-883-3000

Send your content questions/comments to: Christian Wilson wilsonc@byuh.edu

Return to Culture Page

Return to PCC Page

INTEGRATION IDEAS

● Native plants
Have students search the link on native plants to find the plant known as "the symbol of the Pacific" and list its various names. Have students create a database to inventory and compare important plants and plant symbols from their own local and cultural background.

● Compare and contrast
Have students graph and compare the statistical data on each island at this site.

OTHER SITES RELATED TO THIS TOPIC

Polynesian Plants (Biology)
    URL: http://mana.byuh.edu/docs/Plants.htm
Fiji, Hawaii, New Zealand, Samoa, Tahiti, Tonga (Geography)
    URL: http://mana.byuh.edu/docs/Maps.htm
    URL: http://mana.byuh.edu/docs/Geography.htm

KIDS' CORNER

URL: http://www.ot.com/kids/

A must visit for younger students, the Kids' Corner is home to a fun online puzzle, a hangman game, an interesting interactive story, and a large database of links to other Web sites of interest to young children.

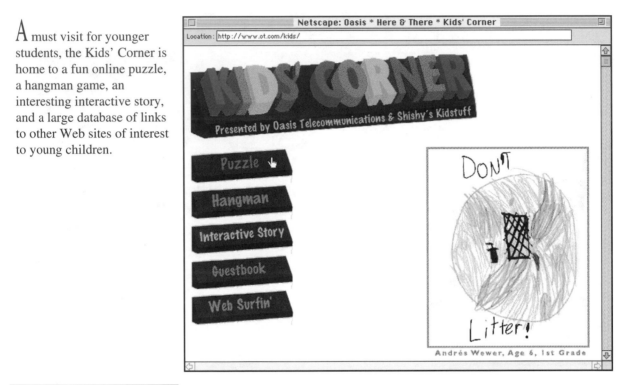

INTEGRATION IDEA

- **Surf lesson**
  Allow students to point and click their way through this site to learn how to use a mouse and to navigate the Web via hyperlinks and browsers.

OTHER SITES RELATED TO THIS TOPIC

BattleShip Online
URL: http://csugrad.cs.vt.edu/htbin/battleship?
Tic Tac Toe on the Web
URL: http://csugrad.cs.vt.edu/~jfink/ttt.html
Uncle Bob's Kids Page
URL: http://rs6.loc.gov/amhome.html

PATHFINDER & TIME MAGAZINE

URL: http://www.pathfinder.com

PathFinder is your interactive link to Time Inc.'s publications, including this week's issue of *Time, Sports Illustrated, Money,* and *Vibe*. It features full-text stories (and a searchable database of past articles) from more than a dozen Time Inc. publications. This is an excellent site students will enjoy visiting to read up on and gather materials for current events-related activities or assignments. The best way to find out about new additions to the site is to subscribe to the free PathFinder Compass online magazine via the following address. **URL: http://www.pathfinder.com/pathfinder/compass/subscribe.html**

INTEGRATION IDEAS

• News ranking
Have students make a list of news stories from the *Time Daily* page and make judgment calls as to their order of importance. Compare the lists with actual news broadcasts and discuss why editors considered some stories more newsworthy than others.

• Email the staff
Go to the Bulletin Boards page and let students post comments and questions about the news coverage of the day to the magazine staff.

OTHER SITES RELATED TO THIS TOPIC

Social Sciences/Humanities (Current Events)
> **URL: gopher://gopher.enews.com:2100/11/**
> **URL: news:clari.news.education**
> **URL: news:clari.news.top**
> **URL: http://www.helsinki.fi/~lsaarine/news.html**

SELF-HELP PSYCHOLOGY MAGAZINE

URL: http://www.well.com/user/selfhelp/

The Self-Help site offers dozens of informative articles "written by mental health professionals and students for the discussion of general psychology." The hyperlinked table of contents will take you to special features, including "Should You Be Concerned About Your Drinking?" Readers will find plenty of informative articles in departments such as Relationships, Parenting and Family Life, Health, Depression and Anxiety, and Addictions and Tobacco. Of special interest are children's movie and software

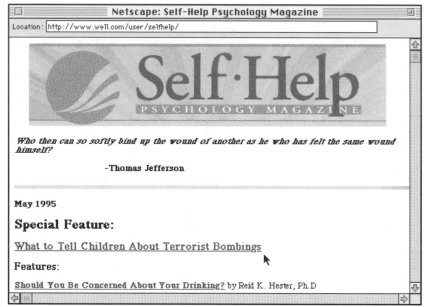

reviews written for parents from a psychological point of view. Each review provides information about potentially harmful content and gives practical advice for helping parents help their children with these themes.

INTEGRATION IDEA

- **General discussion**
  After students visit the site, begin a class discussion about the issues psychologists and psychiatrists work with today. What situations do they encounter that weren't so pervasive a few decades ago? Do students think eating disorders or workplace stress were as prevalent years ago? What about addictions? Talk about environmental versus biological factors.

OTHER SITES RELATED TO THIS TOPIC

American Academy of Child and Adolescent Psychiatry
     URL: http://www.med.umich.edu/aacap/homepage.html
Attention Deficit Disorder
     URL: http://www.seas.upenn.edu/~mengwong/add/
Eating Disorders
     URL: http://ccwf.cc.utexas.edu/~bjackson/UTHealth/eating.html

THOMAS: LEGISLATIVE INFORMATION

URL: http://thomas.loc.gov

The U.S. Congress updates and maintains Thomas, a vast, searchable database of all 1993, 1994, and 1995 House and Senate bills, including summaries and chronologies of pending legislation. You'll also find today's issue of the Congressional Record, email directories for House and Senate members and committees, and C-SPAN transcripts and broadcast schedules. Be sure to have students use the site's fantastic search capabilities.

Netscape: THOMAS: Legislative Information on the Internet

Location: http://thomas.loc.gov/

THOMAS
Legislative Information on the Internet

In the spirit of Thomas Jefferson, a service of the U.S. Congress through its Library.

- **Full Text of Legislation**
  Full text of all versions of House and Senate bills searchable by keyword(s) or by bill number.
    - 103rd Congress
    - 104th Congress

- **Full Text of the Congressional Record**
    - 103rd Congress NEW
    - 104th Congress

INTEGRATION IDEAS

● Track a bill

Have students access Thomas and find several bills pending in the House or Senate. Ask them to choose one to track through the process, using information posted to Thomas daily.

● Constituent email

Access Thomas' list of email addresses for members of Congress. Find the addresses for your state's senators and representatives and have students write letters explaining their views on bills pending in Congress.

OTHER SITES RELATED TO THIS TOPIC

How U.S. Laws Are Made
    URL: http://thomas.loc.gov/home/lawsmade.toc.html
Index to U.S. Government Internet Sites
    URL: http://www.fie.com

U. S. STATE DEPARTMENT TRAVEL ADVISORIES

URL: http://www.stolaf.edu/network/travel-advisories.html

Netscape: U.S. State Department Travel Warnings

Location: http://www.stolaf.edu/network/travel-advisories.html

U.S. State Department Travel Warnings and Consular Information Sheets

Pick a country you would like to visit or research, then head to this home page to learn all sorts of things about it, courtesy of the U.S. State Department. Click on Algeria and you'll discover that the Department of State "warns U.S. citizens to avoid travel to Algeria... continuing attacks against foreigners indicate that the level of risk in Algeria remains high. There is a risk of attack against people traveling overland without adequate security." Maps and flags are included with each entry.

INTEGRATION IDEAS

● Political unrest

Have students browse this site for countries for which the State Department has issued travel warnings, especially countries "in the news." Have them do research to discover what cultural, religious, or political reasons are behind the unrest and give a brief report.

● Keypals

As a long-term project, find a keypal class in a country with a travel advisory. Have students discuss the causes of the advisory and its effect on the lives of the country's citizens and visitors.

OTHER SITES RELATED TO THIS TOPIC

The Xerox Interactive Map
URL: http://pubweb.parc.xerox.com:80/map
The Virtual Tourist Maps
URL: http://wings.buffalo.edu/world
Travel Links
URL: http://www-leland.stanford.edu/~naked/stms.htm

YOUNG PERSON'S GUIDE TO THE INTERNET

URL: http://www.osc.on.ca/kids.html

A great starting point for teachers looking to find sites their younger students will enjoy and learn from. Here you'll find dozens of sites related to just as many curriculum areas—from the Global SchoolHouse to Music sites around the planet.

INTEGRATION IDEAS

● Hotlist lesson

Have your younger students use this site to access the sites listed. Have them create their own personal hotlists of the sites they like best, then exchange them with their classmates so everyone can visit as many sites as possible!

OTHER SITES RELATED TO THIS TOPIC

Scholastic on the Web
URL: http://Scholastic.com:2005
KidLink
URL: http://www.kidlink.org
See & Say Online
URL: http://www.pencom.com/~ph/sas.html

CHAPTER

VOCATIONAL
EDUCATION

- CareerMosaic
- ElNet Galaxy's Workplace Index
- The Entry Level Job Seeker Assistant
- The Internet's Online Career Center
- NCS Career Magazine
- Peterson's Education Center

CAREERMOSAIC

URL: http://www.careermosaic.com

CareerMosaic should be on every high school student's and guidance counselor's hotlist. College-bound students will want to visit The College Connection to see what kind of co-op opportunities and entry-level openings exist for various fields. Students can also go to the Jobs Offered Database, enter keywords related to the professions they want to research, and get valuable information about salary ranges, growth potential, geographic locations, and much more.

INTEGRATION IDEAS

• Diversity
Have students follow links in the Cultural Diversity section to learn about diversity in the workplace. Have them use the Net to find the most up-to-date information on affirmative action, the glass ceiling, and quotas.

• Job search
Have students visit the InfoCenter to find information to guide their job-seeking strategies and resume preparation.

OTHER SITES RELATED TO THIS TOPIC

College Financing, Financial Aid, and Student Loans
    URL: http://www.infi.net/collegemoney/
Financial Aid Information Sources
    URL: http://www-cgi.cs.cmu.edu/afs/cs.cmu.edu/user/mkant/Public/FinAid/finaid.html
U.S. International Job Assistance
    URL: gopher://gopher.indiana.edu/11/theuniversity/life/intlcent

EINET GALAXY'S WORKPLACE INDEX

URL: http://galaxy.einet.net/galaxy/Community/Workplace.html

Yet another valuable and comprehensive resource from EINet Galaxy, this index includes all of the items mentioned elsewhere in this chapter plus hundreds more. Be sure to add this page to your hotlist, load your printer with paper, and set your followed links configuration to "Never Expire" so that you can keep track of each place you jump to from this exhaustive index.

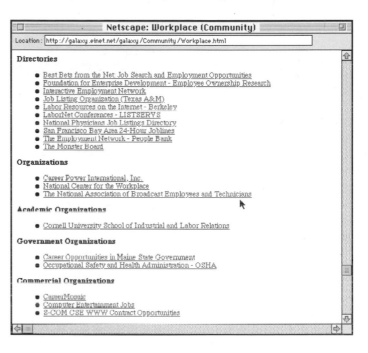

INTEGRATION IDEA

• Research

In preparation for an upcoming research paper or project, have your students look up possible online sources of information on the subject using this Web index.

OTHER SITES RELATED TO THIS TOPIC

Business/Career Resources at Yahoo
   URL: http://www.yahoo.com/Business/
Career Manager
   URL: http://www.espan.com/js/js.html
Career Resource Homepage
   URL: http://www.rpi.edu/dept/cdc/jobsurfer.html

THE ENTRY LEVEL JOB SEEKER ASSISTANT

URL: http://galaxy.einet.net/galaxy/Community/The-Workplace/
joseph-schmalhofer/jobs.html

Besides offering a great index of Internet sites that post job openings, the Entry Level Job Seeker Assistant contains hyperlinks to resources useful to high school students. Click on Resume Links to find categories such as Aerospace Engineering, Business Management, Computer Sciences, Journalism, and Mathematics. Each link contains actual resumes from Internauts seeking employment via the Net. Plenty of links to other Internet resources are included.

```
┌─────────────────────────────────────────────────────────────┐
│ □        Netscape: Entry Level Job Seeker Assistant      ▣   │
├─────────────────────────────────────────────────────────────┤
│ Location : http://galaxy.einet.net/galaxy/Community/The-Workplace/joseph-schmalhofer │
├─────────────────────────────────────────────────────────────┤
│                                                           ⬆  │
│  Welcome to the Entry Level Job                           ▓  │
│        Seeker Assistant!                                      │
│  ─────────────────────────────────────────────────────       │
│                                                              │
│  Dedication                                                  │
│                                                              │
│  This page is dedicated to the assistance of people who have never held a full │
│  time, permanent job in their field, or who have have less than a year of │
│  non-academic experience. Good luck in your search and may this page assist │
│  you.                                                        │
│  ─────────────────────────────────────────────────────       │
│                                                              │
│  Quick Menu                                                  │
│                                                              │
│  This homepage is divided up into 2 parts.                   │
│                                                              │
│    ● Job Links                                               │
│    ● Resume Links                                         ⬇  │
│  ◁─────────────────────────────────────────────────────▷     │
└─────────────────────────────────────────────────────────────┘
```

INTEGRATION IDEAS

● Role playing
Download resumes from several fields to display on an overhead projector. Have the class analyze them as if they were employers, picking out winning resumes, good resumes, and those needing improvement.

● Resume dissection
Have each student pick a potential career and read the resumes for that field. What skills does the job require? How do job seekers package their assets and talents?

OTHER SITES RELATED TO THIS TOPIC

American Institute of Physics Career Bulletin Board
URL: http://www.aip.org/aip/careers/careers.html
Scholary Societies Project
URL: http://www.lib.uwaterloo.ca/society/overview.html
Career Development Resources from the American Mathematical Society
URL: gopher://e-math.ams.org/11/profInfo/Career.Devel

THE INTERNET'S ONLINE CAREER CENTER

URL: http://occ.com

Welcome to one of the most popular stops on the World Wide Web. Most traffic comes from Internauts who browse the extensive job listings, but the site also features valuable resources for teachers and students. The On-Campus section links students with information on dozens of colleges on the Net. Then it's a quick jump to The Kaplan Educational Centers for information about career planning and SATs. The Career Assistance area contains career advice articles from nationally-recognized columnists and other valuable resources. The site also includes links to professional associations and numerous cultural diversity resources.

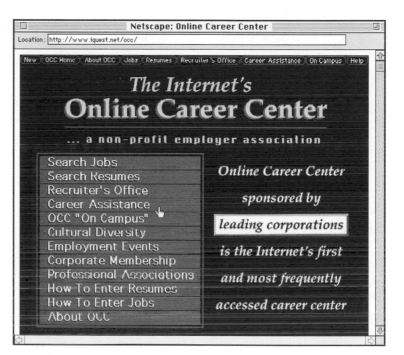

INTEGRATION IDEAS

• Job search
Have students select a field and look for job openings. Have them write cover letters and create resumes, and challenge them to "apply" to their classmates, who will critique their work.

• Online resumes
Have students use the "Search Resumes" area and find online resumes related to their fields. How do they compare with those students created in the first exercise?

OTHER SITES RELATED TO THIS TOPIC

Jobs newsgroups:

URL: news:bionet.jobs **URL: news:biz.jobs.offered**

URL: news:misc.jobs.resumes **URL: news:misc.jobs.offered.entry**

World Wide Web Resume Bank

URL: http://www.careermag.com/careermag/resumes/index.html

NCS CAREER MAGAZINE

URL: http://www.careermag.com/careermag/

The NCS Career Magazine is a tremendous resource for students thinking about their future endeavors. Start by clicking the News and Articles button, and you'll soon find features such as "Resume Rules and Regulations: How to Win the Game" and "Salary and Employment Survey Findings." Scroll down to find an extensive index of articles on interviewing, networking, research and preparation, and resume writing. Be sure to check out "The Best of The Wall Street Journal's National Business Employment Weekly." In the Career-Related Links section you'll find pointers to other online resources, including Industry-Specific Job Information at Ohio State University.

INTEGRATION IDEA

● Global contact

Let students participate in the Career Forum, where they can communicate with people around the world on topics such as interviewing, workplace environment, legal issues, and the economy's effect on employment.

OTHER SITES RELATED TO THIS TOPIC

Welcome to the Monster Board!
   URL: http://199.94.216.71:81/home.html
Catapult Career and Employment Resources
   URL: http://www.wm.edu/catapult/catapult.html
Incorporating the Internet Into Your Job Search Strategy
   URL: http://www.wpi.edu/Depts/Library/jobguide/what-now.html

PETERSON'S EDUCATION CENTER

URL: http://www.petersons.com:8080

The Peterson's Education Center is the place to go to search for information on student financial aid or for details on more than 3,300 accredited undergraduate institutions. Students looking for advice on selecting the right vocational technology institution will find a complete catalogue of information on hundreds of U.S. schools. One neat feature is Peterson's guide to Summer Programs, which provides information on programs offered by more than 1,400 organizations

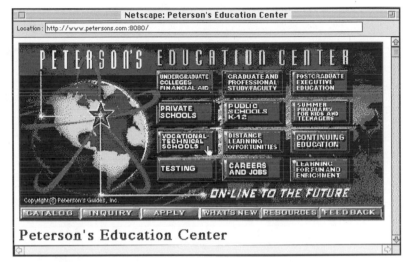

Peterson's Education Center

ranging from camps to private colleges. Scan by alphabetical, geographical, or topical index, or use the site's handy search feature to enter keywords matching your interests.

INTEGRATION IDEAS

• Financial aid

Have students use this site to find at least five possible sources of financial aid that fit their family and income situation.

• Test preparation

Have students getting ready for SATs or LSATs visit the Testing area for tips and guides to successful test taking.

OTHER SITES RELATED TO THIS TOPIC

Online Occupational Outlook Handbook
        URL: gopher://umslvma.umsl.edu/11/library/stacks/books/ooha
Career Power International
        URL: http://netmart.com:80/ak.html

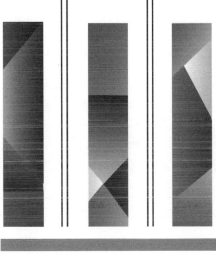

APPENDIX

QUESTIONS & ANSWERS
ABOUT THE
WORLD WIDE WEB

Whether you're a first-time visitor to the Web or an old hand, there's always something new to learn about it. Why? Because it's growing and evolving by leaps and bounds every day. The following question and answer appendix covers the basic facts of this new technology. New Web and Internet terms we introduce will appear in italics.

This section also gives you details about software and other resources that will help you make the most out of the Web at your school. So, if you already know what URL and other basics mean, just skip through the questions until you find one that is helpful to you. And if you think this Q & A section will be useful when you teach educators or students about the Web, we give you permission to use this appendix for educational purposes. All we ask is that you note the following: "Excerpted from the *Educator's World Wide Web TourGuide*, with the permission of the publishers of *Classroom Connect*, (717) 393-1000."

What is the World Wide Web ?

The World Wide Web (or WWW or Web for short) is simply one small part of the *Internet,* the world's largest computer network. The Internet spans 160 countries and connects millions of computers to each other. More than 30 million people use "the Net" to communicate with one another, exchange and browse through online libraries of information, and retrieve useful software and documents.

The Web is the fastest growing and easiest-to-use part of the Internet. That's because it allows computer users to use their mouse to point-and-click their way through the Internet's text, graphics, sounds, and video clips— and to view them on the screen at the same time. In fact, the Web could be considered a CD-ROM-like method of accessing Internet information.

The Web's combination of online media drives the Internet's exploding growth, and finally makes the Net's rich information resources easy to navigate and use in the classroom. (See figures 1.1 and 1.2 for a comparison of the Internet before and after the Web was developed.)

```
┌─────────────── fedworld.gov 1 ───────────────┐
│ * MajorTCP/IP by Vircom Inc. *                │
│                                               │
│    ***************************************    │
│    *                                     *    │
│    *   Welcome to the FedWorld Information Network!  *    │
│    *                                     *    │
│    ***************************************    │
│                                               │
│   The following destinations are available... │
│                                               │
│   [1] FedWorld                                │
│                                               │
│   [2] IRIS - IRS Tax forms, Publications and Information │
│                                               │
│   [X] Abort Connection                        │
│                                               │
│ Please select an option from above and press <return>:  1▮ │
└───────────────────────────────────────────────┘
```

Figure 1.1

Before the World Wide Web, all Internet information was text-based. Users had to memorize cryptic commands and type them into their computers to get around online and to access information.

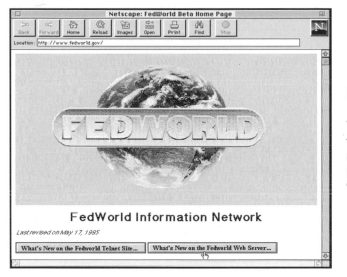

Figure 1.2

With the Web, a user need only point and click with a mouse to sample all of the text, graphics, sounds, and video clips on the Internet. They can be accessed at the same time through a colorful, CD-ROM-like interface.

How does the Web work

Think of the World Wide Web as a spider's web of computer connections spanning the globe via the Internet. After you sign on to the Net, you load special software (called a *Web browser*, which we'll cover in a moment) and begin navigating the Web. When you access a computer on the Web, your computer screen fills with a *Web page* full of information. You can navigate through information stored on any other Internet-connected computer, instantly, simply by pointing and clicking on text or graphics on your computer screen.

For example, you can access a Web document about baroque music on a computer in Germany, and then "link" to related information contained on another Web computer in the United States. Moving through related information leads to more Web pages with links to data at other sites.

Without your realizing it, your computer may have taken you on a tour of dozens of computers all over the globe in just a few minutes simply by your clicking on highlighted words or pictures. The highlighted words or pictures (normally blue in color) are called *hyperlinks,* and are one of the major reasons the Web is so easy to navigate. Whenever you see a blue word or a picture with a blue border on a Web page, you click on it with your mouse (the mouse arrow usually turns into a little hand when you point it at a hyperlink), thus activating a computer command hidden behind the word or picture that reads something like: "If I'm clicked, take this person to a Web page located somewhere else." The link takes you to that page directly, without your having to know where it's located, and displays it to you in seconds. The act of swimming through Web information in this way is known as *browsing* or *surfing.*

What is hypertext and why is it important to the Web

The mechanism that allows Internet users to browse through information on the WWW is called *hypertext.* Think of hypertext as regular text on steroids. It's pretty much the same as normal text in that it can be read, searched, edited, and stored, but with one incredible difference: *hypertext has links within the text to other, related documents located on Internet computers that span the globe.*

Let's backtrack a minute. Remember that document about baroque music we mentioned a few seconds ago? If you were reading that document in hypertext (Web) form, you could select the blue, highlighted word **music** using your mouse. After clicking on it, one or more documents related to the word would appear before you—perhaps a definition of the word or a list of famous composers and musicians. These new documents would have links within them which would connect you to other documents.

But hypertext documents don't contain only text. They can also include other forms of media—pictures, sounds, and even video clips. The combination of hypertext with these types of multimedia forms creates something called *hypermedia.* Here's an example of hypermedia: You could be reading a Web document about the Japanese language and click on a phrase in the hypertext to hear it spoken. Or, if you were browsing the Web version of an art gallery, you could click on a sculpture and view a computer-generated movie of it rotating. By controlling the movie, you could even zoom in to see greater detail or zoom out to see the other objects around it.

The Web and the Internet—aren't they the same thing ?

It's important to recognize that the World Wide Web is *not* the Internet. The Web merely uses the Internet to transmit hypertext Web documents between computers. Of course, the Web wouldn't be possible *without* the Internet. But many people are able to use the Internet without using the Web. They may use other Internet navigation tools such as email, gopher, or telnet.

How does the World Wide Web work ?

In Internet lingo, the Web works using what's known as the *client-server model.* (Brace yourself for some techie talk here.) All computers on the Internet containing Web pages run a special program called a *Web server* that, when asked, "serves" information to other computers. The server is often called a *Web site.* A WWW client (Web browser software) is a software program on your computer that requests information from a Web server.

Here's a quick example of how the client-server process works: After loading a Web browser program, an Internet user connects to a Web site, retrieves a Web page, and selects a hyperlink. The link might be "1990 Census data for Michigan," for example. The browser then connects to a computer somewhere on the WWW and asks that computer's Web server for "1990 Census data for Michigan." The server then responds by sending the information (whether it be hypertext or some other hypermedia) to the user's (client's) screen. As you read this, thousands of these client-server transactions are taking place all over the world, creating a web of information that's constantly flowing, day and night.

Now I understand what the Web is, how it works, and what hypertext is all about. But what does the HTTP that I see on Web addresses mean ?

The computer language that Web clients and servers use to talk to each other is known as *Hypertext Transmission Protocol,* or *HTTP.* Web clients and servers must be able to speak in HTTP to transmit and receive hypertext and hypermedia files. Thus, as you page through this book, you'll notice that all of the Web site addresses begin with **http://**. This is the first thing you type into your Web browser as you prepare to visit a new Web site, letting the software know that it has to use Hypertext Transport Protocol to get the information. After the **http://** you type the name of the computer you're accessing, and then perhaps the subdirectory and the file you want to pull up. Whenever you see **http**, you know the site is on the Web.

> For example:
> **http://www.wentworth.com/classroom/edulinks.htm**

Many Web site addresses in this book begin with the letters URL. What do they mean

URL stands for *Uniform Resource Locator*. It's what the Web uses to indicate the location of information on the Internet. It's possible to represent almost any file or computer on the Internet using a URL, even if the file is not a Web page. (See *Internet tools via the Web*.) The first portion of a URL represents the Internet navigational software used to access a piece of information. The middle portion is usually the address of the computer where the data or computer is located. The final portion may be the name of an individual file.

URL: **http://www.wentworth.com/classroom/edulinks.htm**

In the above address, the **http** tells the Web computers what language to use to communicate. The **www.wentworth.com** is the address of the computer where the data or computer file is stored. The **classroom** portion is the name of the subdirectory where the file *edulinks.htm* is located. A URL is always in the form of a single unbroken line containing no spaces.

▼▼▼ Internet tools via the Web ▼▼▼

URLs make the Web amazingly flexible. You can use the World Wide Web to use all the other Internet tools: email, gopher, telnet, file transfer protocol (ftp), and newsgroups. Here are some examples of what you could do if you typed in some of the following URLs.

http://www.eff.org
> Would connect you to the Electronic Frontier Foundation's Web server. The **http://** prefix tells you this is a Web site.

ftp://ftp.wentworth.com/wentworth/Classroom-Connect/Incite95.txt
> Would access the public hard drive on *Classroom Connect's* computer and download (or retrieve) the file *Incite95.txt* directly to your computer. The **ftp://** prefix tells you this is an ftp site.

gopher://wiretap.spies.com
> Would open a gopher, or menu-based, Internet session with this computer.

Continued on next page

telnet://pac.carl.org
> Would open a telnet, or interactive, session with this computer.

mailto:user@computer.edu
> Would send an email message to this Internet user.

wais://Bible.src
> Would open a WAIS (Wide Area Information Server) session with this document.

news:alt.computers
> Would allow you to read messages posted to this Usenet newsgroup.

How are schools using the Web ?

The short answer is that the Web is opening up the Internet to students for the first time, enabling them to communicate with distant peers and access libraries of information they never dreamed existed—all via a user-friendly, colorful interface. For a longer, more comprehensive answer, see the Preface and Introduction to find out how the Web is being used in education.

Where did the Web come from ?

The Web's history can be traced back to 1989, when a team of physicists in Europe began developing a new way to share their research via the Internet. They had grown tired of sending their graphical data and research to each other in text-only form, and wanted a new way to present their information online to each other in real time, graphically.

The Web left the realm of science and became accessible to rest of the world when graphical Web browsers such as Mosaic, a free software program distributed across the Internet to anyone who wanted it, were developed. Mosaic allowed users to access the World Wide Web and the graphical documents stored on it. While the first documents were put on the Web by researchers, like many tools on the Internet, users began to find new uses for the technology. Today the Web has millions of documents housed in computers at every corner of the globe. Mosaic is still one of the most powerful WWW browsers available, second only to NetScape, a relative newcomer to the Web browser world.

Here is a brief rundown of what users can do with today's graphical Web browsers:

- Use a friendly, mouse-driven interface to access Internet information.
- Display hypertext and hypermedia documents on the Web, formatted into several fonts in regular, bold, or italic typefaces in different colors.
- Connect to hypertext and hypermedia links, and keep a running record of hyperlinks that have been explored. This is called a *history list.*
- Keep a permanent list of favorite Web sites that users can click on to access in a second. This is called a *hotlist* or *bookmarks.*

- Display character sets for many languages.
- Display or retrieve pictures, sounds, and movies, and then play them on the screen.
- Fill out electronic forms via blank fields, buttons, or check boxes.
- Use keywords to search for specific information located on the Internet.

Why are Web browsers sometimes called "killer" applications ?

To many Internet users, their Web browser has come to replace all other Internet navigational software—they've all been "killed" in favor of this new program.

Thanks to Mosaic and NetScape, users no longer need to load up separate and distinct programs for browsing the Internet. They can handle gopher, telnet, ftp (file transfer protocol), WAIS, and email, all via a single program.

How can I get on the Web ?

There are three ways educators and their students can gain access to the World Wide Web (and the Internet):

- Via a commercial online service such as America Online, Prodigy, and CompuServe. You must subscribe and pay a monthly and sometimes hourly fee;
- Through a direct Internet hookup using a modem. This is known as a *SLIP or PPP connection;*
- Directly through your school's computer network.

If you're lucky enough to have Internet access through your school's existing computer network, talk with your technology coordinator or librarian about how to bring a Web connection into your classroom. If you're not lucky enough to have Internet access directly through your school, you may need to start from ground zero. The first thing you'll need is a computer, a modem (a 28.8 baud modem is best) and a phone line to connect to the modem. Once you have this equipment, it's time to consider how best to get onto the Internet, and thus, the Web.

The three largest national online services—America Online, Prodigy, and CompuServe—all offer Web browser software to surf the Web. The software is available free to their subscribers and allows them to access all of the Web's holdings.

🏠 Home ⬅ Back ➡ Forward 🔄 Reload ✓ Load Images ⏹ Stop 🔄 Load Original

Current URL: http://www.wentworth.com/classroom/

Page complete   Image complete

Figure 1.3

America Online's Web browser is easy to use, reasonably fast, and free to subscribers. But once America Online members go over their free five hours of usage a month, they're charged for every hour they're online. That can add up to big bucks over a month's time. The same is true for all of the commercial services offering Web access.

Compared to running a browser on your own computer, the Web browsers offered by commercial services are fairly slow in retrieving information from the Web. Because commercial online services charge for access to the Web by the hour, costs can be prohibitive to many schools. (See figure 1.3.) Still, as an interim step to full Internet connectivity, any of these service's Web browsers will work just fine. They're also a great way for individual educators with home computers to give the Net and the Web a try.

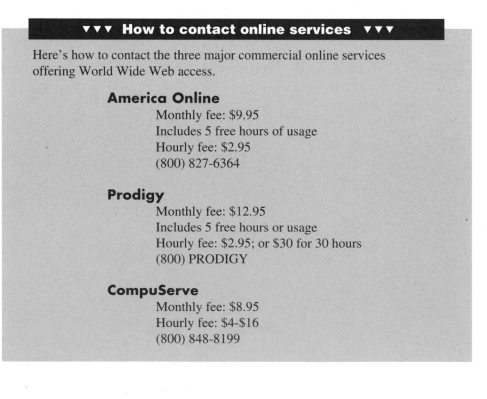

▼▼▼ How to contact online services ▼▼▼

Here's how to contact the three major commercial online services offering World Wide Web access.

America Online
> Monthly fee: $9.95
> Includes 5 free hours of usage
> Hourly fee: $2.95
> (800) 827-6364

Prodigy
> Monthly fee: $12.95
> Includes 5 free hours or usage
> Hourly fee: $2.95; or $30 for 30 hours
> (800) PRODIGY

CompuServe
> Monthly fee: $8.95
> Hourly fee: $4-$16
> (800) 848-8199

I've tried America Online, Prodigy, and CompuServe's Web browsers, but they seem slow and cost too much. How else can I get on the Web

The best way to get on the World Wide Web is to obtain a direct, graphical connection to the Internet, known as a *SLIP (Serial Line Internet Protocol)* or *PPP (Point to Point) connection*. A local Internet service provider can provide you and your classroom with this kind of connection for $20 to $40 per month, and usually with no hourly fees. These rates vary, and many providers offer substantial discounts to schools. Best of all, most service providers allow users to access the Net using 14.4 or 28.8 baud modems, which is more than 10 times the speed of the commercial online services.

Once you purchase a SLIP or PPP connection, your provider will give you the basic software you need to get onto the Internet via your new, direct link. Among those navigation tools should be a Web browser. If one is not included, read on to find out where to get the latest browser software. The browsers MacWeb and WinWeb are also included on the CD-ROM at the back of this book.

▼▼▼ How to find Internet service providers ▼▼▼

There are several ways to obtain a list of service providers in your area.

- Call *Classroom Connect* at **(800) 638-1639**.
- If you're already on the Web through a commercial service, you can also download an extensive list of providers using ftp.
  URL: ftp://ftp.wentworth.com/wentworth/Service.Providers.txt
- Head to your local bookstore and look in the Computer section under Internet. You'll find dozens of books, many containing large lists of local Internet service providers.

What software is available to surf the Web, and where can I get a copy

The CD-ROM at the back of this book includes MacWeb and WinWeb (see below). Several free Web browsers are available to people who use the Internet via a direct Internet connection. Some require a payment when you register the software. Here is a list of those browsers, a brief description, and where to get a copy online.

NetScape Navigator
Available for Mac and Windows, NetScape is the most powerful, easy-to-use Web browser on the Internet. This software is already used by thousands of schools worldwide, and has become the de facto Web browser for millions of Internet users.
Ftp to: ftp.mcom.com
Go to the *netscape* subdirectory

Mosaic

The original Web browser available from the National Center for Supercomputing Applications (NCSA) for Mac and Windows. Not as advanced as NetScape, but every bit as fast.

Ftp to: ftp.ncsa.uiuc.edu

Go to the *Mosaic* subdirectory

MacWeb & WinWeb

Innovative Web browsers developed by the EINet Corporation, MacWeb (Mac) and WinWeb (Windows) are robust, speedy Web browsers that match Mosaic in terms of features and stability. These are included on the CD-ROM at the back of this book.

Ftp to: ftp.einet.net

Go to the *einet* subdirectory

After retrieving this software, you'll notice that it's in compressed form. That means the data have been squeezed together for easier transmission. Before you use the program, the data must be uncompressed using special software. If you're never uncompressed a file before, chances are you'll need uncompression software, which you can find online at the following locations.

Macintosh Expander
Ftp to: ftp.wentworth.com

Go to the *wentworth/Internet-Software/Mac* subdirectory and retrieve the *Expander!.sea* file. Double-click it, and it will automatically uncompress itself.

IBM PC Unzip
Ftp to: ftp.wentworth.com

Go to the *wentworth/Internet-Software/IBM* subdirectory and retrieve the *pkunzip.exe* file.

Use this software to uncompress your Web software. Once that's done, sign on to the Net, load the browser, and start surfing! All of the browsers include help files if you need assistance.

Great! My software is letting me surf the Web. But why can't I listen to sounds or view online video clips ?

That's because the browser software needs *players,* special software that allows you to access the online media you'll find on the Web. Here's where to get copies of the sound, graphic, and video players from the Internet.

Macintosh Web Media Players
Ftp to: ftp.wentworth.com

Go to the *wentworth/Internet-Software/Mac* subdirectory and retrieve the *Web-Viewers.sea* file. (See figure 1.4.) Double-click it, and the players will automatically expand onto your hard drive.

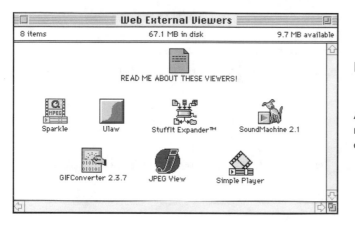

Figure 1.4

All of the Mac software necessary to play multimedia files found on the Web can be found on the **ftp.wentworth.com** site in a single archive.

IBM PC Web Media Players
Ftp to: ftp.ncsa.uiuc.edu

Go to the *Mosaic/Windows/viewers* subdirectory and download the files found here.

I've stumbled across a lot of great information on the Web.
But how can I find education sites and resources I can really use ?

Probably the best way to use your valuable time on the Web is to do a keyword search for sites fitting the subject you have in mind, such as Mark Twain or the Big Bang. A variety of *search tools* or *engines* have been developed to help Web users do this. *Classroom Connect* has assembled all of the best, most comprehensive search tools for the Internet and put them on a single Web page for your use. (See figure 1.5.)

URL: http://www.wentworth.com/classroom/search.htm

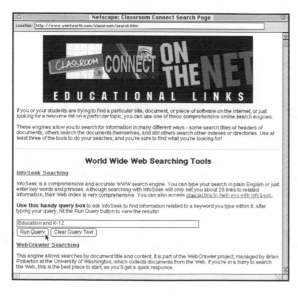

Figure 1.5

The *Classroom Connect* Search Page is home to all of the Net's powerful searching tools. It's the only Internet address you'll ever need to know to find something anywhere online.

I've seen schools with their own pages on the World Wide Web. How do I make my own Web pages ❓

Good question! There are many great online answers. Visit these sites to find basic information and tutorials.

Web Page Basics
> **URL: http://www.emedia.net/pointers/html.html**

A Beginner's Guide to Making Web Pages
> **URL: http://www.ncsa.uiuc.edu/General/Internet/WWW/HTMLPrimer.html**

How to Make a Web Server with a Macintosh
> **URL: http://www.acu.edu/dev/makeaserver.html**

Web66 Classroom Internet Web Server Cookbook (See figure 1.6.)
> **URL: http://web66.coled.umn.edu**

```
┌─────────────────────────────────────────────────┐
│        Netscape: Web 66: Cookbook                 │
├─────────────────────────────────────────────────┤
│ Location: http://web66.coled.umn.edu/Cookbook/contents.html │
├─────────────────────────────────────────────────┤
│  [66]  Classroom Internet Server Cookbook         │
│                                                    │
│ If you entered Web66 here, you might want to visit the Web66 Home Page. │
│                                                    │
│ Written by Stephen E. Collins.                    │
│                                                    │
│ This is cookbook gives the recipes for setting up an Internet server in a classroom. │
│                                                    │
│ Getting Started                                    │
│   1. Your Internet kitchen                         │
│   2. Some Internet kitchen utensils                │
│                                                    │
│ Basic Recipes                                      │
│ If you complete this basic recipe section you will have a fully operational World Wide Web and E-mail │
│ Server.                                            │
│   1. MacHTTP: A World Wide Web Server             │
│   2. HTML: The Eight Minute HTML Primer           │
│   3. Putting pictures on your pages               │
│   4. Putting Sounds on your pages                 │
│   5. MailShare: A Mail Server                     │
└─────────────────────────────────────────────────┘
```

Figure 1.6

The Web66 home page features a nice set of tutorials for educators who want to learn how to create Web pages—even install and set up a Web server.

Our students have made a great Web page for our school, but we don't have the technology in our building to place it on the Web. What can we do ❓

Free Web space is only an email message away. *Classroom Connect's* World Wide Web site has a special place for K-12 educators to mount Web pages from their school—free!

Our ClassroomWeb is the place to display the work of your students and your entire school on the global Internet. We created this free space because many teachers tell us that their school doesn't have a Net-connected computer or the money to place Web pages online. Many students make Web pages as part of school projects, but have no place to put them online for the rest of the world to see.

Any school can submit up to two 8 1/2 x 11-inch Web pages, formatted in Hypertext Markup Language (HTML) with up to two GIF images per page (50k or less each). Send a disk with your pages and graphics by postal mail to Wentworth Worldwide Media, or attach them to an email message.

Send email to Dennis Shirk.
>   *Email to:* **classweb@wentworth.com**

Type **School Web Page** in the subject line, and put your school's name, teacher's name, address, phone number, and email address in the message. To send via postal mail, submit your pages by regular mail in any format (Mac or Windows) to: *Classroom Connect*, Attn: Dennis Shirk, P.O. Box 10488, Lancaster, PA 17605-0488.

We'll place the Web pages we receive in this directory on our Web site, accessible via the following address:

>   **URL: http://www.wentworth.com/classweb**

When I've got a question or need help with something about the Web, where can I go for help online, and in the real world ?

The Web features plenty of great sources of information to help you get on the Web and successfully navigate its resources. Here is a list of books and online sources of basic Web information.

Classroom Connect Newsletter
Wentworth Worldwide Media
$39

Educator's Internet Companion: Classroom Connect's Complete Guide to Educational Resources on the Internet
Wentworth Worldwide Media
$40

Hands-On Mosaic: A Tutorial for Windows Users
Prentice Hall
$29

Instant Internet with Websurfer
Prentice Hall
$24

Mosaic Quick Tour for Mac & Windows
Ventana Press
$12

169

NetScape Quick Tour for Mac & Windows
Ventana Press
$14

The Mosaic Handbook for Microsoft Windows
O'Reilly & Associates
$34

The Mosaic Navigator
John Wiley & Sons, Inc.
$17

The World Wide Web Unleashed
Sams Publishing
$45

Entering the World Wide Web: A Guide to Cyberspace
> **URL: http://www.hcc.hawaii.edu/guide/www.guide.html**

Starting Points for Web Navigation
> **URL: http://www.ncsa.uiuc.edu/SDG/Software/Mosaic/StartingPoints/
> NetworkStartingPoints.html**

The World Wide Web's Original Home in Switzerland
> **URL: http://www.w3.org/hypertext/WWW/LineMode/Defaults/
> default.html**

World Wide Web Frequently Asked Questions (FAQ) File
> **URL: http://sunsite.unc.edu/boutell/faq/www_faq.html**

World Wide Web Starter Kit Online
> **URL: http://www.state.ut.us/webinfo/**

Classroom Connect
> **URL: http://www.wentworth.com**

GLOSSARY

WORLD WIDE WEB AND INTERNET GLOSSARY

Bookmarks (See *Hotlist*)

Browser (See *Web browser*)

Bulletin board service (BBS) A forum for users to browse and exchange information. Computer BBSs are accessible by telephone via a personal computer and a modem. Many BBSs are small operations run by a single person that allow only several users to log on at the same time. Some are much larger and allow hundreds of users to login simultaneously to use the system. Huge, commercial examples are America Online, CompuServe, and Prodigy.

Client-server model The computerized system that makes the Web work. All computers on the Internet containing Web pages run a special program called a Web server that, when asked, "serves" information to Internet users. A WWW client (Web browser software) is a program that requests information from a Web server.

Commercial online service A company that, for a fee, allows computer users to dial in via modem to access its information and services, which can include Internet and Web access. Examples are America Online, CompuServe, Delphi, and Prodigy.

Database A computer holding large amounts of information that can be searched by an Internet user. A storehouse of information on the Net.

Dial-up Internet connection Lets a user dial into an Internet service provider using a modem and telephone line to access the Internet. The user is presented with a text-based set of menus which are used to navigate the Internet. (See **SLIP** or **PPP connections**)

Directory A list of files or other directories on a computer at an Internet site.

Download/upload To download is to transfer a file from another computer to the user's computer. To upload is to send a file to another computer.

Email Allows users to send and receive messages to each other over the Internet.

File transfer protocol (ftp) Allows files to be transferred between Internet-connected computers.

Frequently Asked Questions (FAQ) FAQ files answer frequently asked questions on hundreds of Internet- and Web-related topics. They're freely available at many locations on the Net. This site holds every FAQ on the Net. A World Wide Web FAQ can be found on the CD-ROM included with this book.
Ftp to: **rtfm.mit.edu**
Go to the *pub/usenet/news.answers* subdirectory

Gopher A menu-based system for browsing Internet information.

Graphical interface Software that allows Internet users to execute commands and navigate through online information by pointing and clicking on words or phrases with a mouse.

Home page The first page that appears when accessing a World Wide Web site. The home page is essentially the table of contents to a Web site.

Hotlist A personal list of favorite Web addresses, organized in a single list. All Web browsers allow users to create hotlists so users can return to their favorite Web sites. Also known as **Bookmarks**.

HTML (Hypertext Markup Language) Easy to learn "programming" language for the World Wide Web. HTML turns text files into Web documents by embedding small style codes into the text to change fonts, colors, sizes, and placement of text, pictures, sounds, or video clips. An HTML primer course can be found here.
URL: http://sunsite.unc.edu/boutell/faq/www_faq.html

HTTP (Hypertext Transport Protocol) The computer language Web clients (browser software) and servers (Web sites) use to transmit information to and from each other.

Hyperlink A highlighted blue word or graphic in a Web page that, when clicked with a mouse, takes Internet users to a related piece of information somewhere on the Internet.

Hypermedia The images (pictures), sound files, and video clips accessible on the World Wide Web.

Hypertext The mechanism that allows Internet users to browse through information on the Web. Web pages are created with hypertext and contain links to other Web documents or resources located on Internet computers.

Internaut Anyone who uses the Internet.

Internet The global "network of networks" that connects more than three million computers (called hosts). The Internet is the virtual "space" in which users send and receive email, login to remote computers (telnet), browse databases of information (gopher, World Wide Web, WAIS), and send and receive programs (ftp) contained on these computers.

Internet account Purchased through an Internet service provider, the account assigns a password and email address to an individual or group.

Internet Relay Chat (IRC) Interactive, real-time discussions between Internauts using text messages. Users log onto designated Net computers and join discussions already in progress. More information about IRC can be obtained via ftp.
Ftp to: **cs-ftp.bu.edu**
Go to the *irc/support* subdirectory

Internet server A computer that stores data that can be accessed via the Internet.

Internet Service Provider (ISP) Any organization that provides access to the Internet. Many ISPs also offer technical assistance to schools looking to become Internet information providers by placing their school's information online. They also help schools get connected to the Net. A list of ISPs can be retrieved via ftp.
Ftp to: **ftp.wentworth.com**
Look in the *wentworth* subdirectory

Internet site A computer connected to the Internet containing information that can be accessed using an Internet navigation tool such as ftp, telnet, gopher, or a Web browser.

IP address Every computer on the Internet has a unique numerical IP (Internet Protocol) address assigned to it, such as 123.456.78.9.

Keyword A word or words which can be searched for in documents or menus.

Logon To sign on to a computer system.

Mailing list (or Listserv) More than 4,000 topic-oriented, email-based message bases that can be read and posted to. Users subscribe to the lists they want to read and receive messages via email. Mailing lists are operated using listserv software. Thus, many Internauts call mailing lists "listserver." There are two types of lists: moderated and unmoderated. Moderated lists are screened by a human before being posted to subscribers. Messages to unmoderated lists are automatically forwarded to subscribers.

Menu A list of information that leads to documents or other menus.

Modem An electronic device that attaches to a computer and links that computer to the online world via a phone line. Modems are available for any computer, can be internal or external, and come in several speeds, known as the baud rate. The higher the baud rate, the faster the modem. The most popular modem speed has been 14,000 baud, but 28,800 baud modems are now considered the standard. Most Internet service providers allow you to dial into their systems at 14,400, or even 28,800 baud.

Mosaic The original Web browser software available from the National Center for Supercomputing Applications (NCSA) for both Mac and Windows. Not as advanced as NetScape, but every bit as fast.
Ftp to: **ftp.ncsa.uiuc.edu**
Go to the *Mosaic* subdirectory

NetScape Available for both Mac and Windows, NetScape is the most powerful, easy-to-use Web browser on the Internet. This software is already in use by thousands of schools worldwide, and has become the de facto Web browser for millions of Internet users.
Ftp to: ftp.mcom.com
Go to the *netscape* subdirectory

Net surfer Someone who browses the Internet with no definite destination.

Network A group of computers that are connected in some fashion. Most school networks are known as LANs, or Local Area Networks, because they are networks linking computers in one small area. The Internet could be referred to as a WAN, or a Wide Area Network, because it connects computers in more than one local area.

Online/Offline When you are logged onto a computer through your modem, you are said to be online. When you're using your computer but are not connected to another computer through your modem, you're said to be working offline.

Posts Email messages sent to a mailing list or Usenet newsgroup to be read by subscribers or others on the Internet.

Search engine An Internet site that allows for keyword searching of online information. Most of the Internet's search engines can be accessed through a single Web page.
URL: http://www.wentworth.com/classroom/search.htm

SLIP (Serial Line Internet Protocol) or PPP (Point to Point Protocol) Internet connections Both allow a computer to connect to the Internet with a modem and telephone line. Users can then navigate the Internet using graphical (Web) software on their computer. This is in contrast to using a Dial-up Internet connection, in which a user is forced to navigate the Net using a text-based set of menus.

Telnet Allows users to access computers and their data at thousands of places around the world, most often at libraries, universities, and government agencies.

Text-based Internet account The user must type Unix commands to navigate the Internet.

URL (Universal Resource Locator) The address and method used to locate a specific resource on the Internet. A URL beginning with **http://** indicates that the site is a Web resource and that a Web browser must be used to access it. Internauts can also use URLs to access gopher, ftp, and telnet sites, to send email, and to view newsgroup postings.

Usenet newsgroups More than 11,000 topic-oriented message bases that can be read and posted to. Also called newsgroups.

Virtual A computer-generated environment.

WWW Abbreviation for the World Wide Web.

175

WAIS (Wide Area Information Servers) These servers allow users to conduct full-text keyword searches in documents, databases, and libraries connected to the Internet.

Web Short for World Wide Web.

Web browser Software that allows Internet users to access and navigate the World Wide Web. Some Web browsers, such as NetScape and Mosaic, are graphical. Lynx is a text-based browser used on Unix computers.

Web page A single online document containing information that can be accessed over the World Wide Web.

World Wide Web (WWW or Web) A revolutionary Internet browsing system that allows for point-and-click navigation of the Internet. The WWW is a spiderweb-like interconnection of millions of pieces of information located on computers around the world. Web documents use hypertext, which incorporates text and graphical "links" to other documents and files on Internet-connected computers.

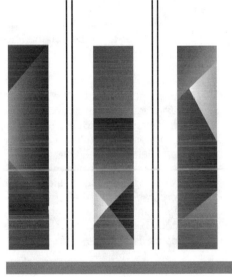

SITE LIST

CHAPTER 1
Art

CHAPTER 2
Business

CHAPTER 3
English/Literature

CHAPTER 4
Foreign Languages

CHAPTER 5
Geography

CHAPTER 6
Health/Physical Education

CHAPTER 7
History

CHAPTER 8
Mathematics

CHAPTER 9
Science

CHAPTER 10
Social Sciences/ Humanities

CHAPTER 11
Vocational Education

COLOR SECTION

Art

Anima Media Arts
Fractal Movie Archive
The Louvre

Business

Radio HK Internet Radio

English/Literature

Bartlett's Familiar Passages, Phrases, and Proverbs
The Electric Postcard
The Froggy Page
Online Children's Books
Pathfinder
Theodore Tugboat

Foreign Languages

Asia Online
French Language Web
Intercultural E-Mail Classroom Connections

Geography

European Home Page
Virtual Tourist World Map

Health/
Physical Education

Hippocrates
International Food Information Council
National Parent Information Network

History

Anti-Imperialism in the United States, 1898-1935
Civil War Photographs

Mathematics

Ask Dr. Math
Blue Dog
Mathematics & Molecules K-12
MegaMath
The Explorer

Science

Centre for Atmospheric Science
CU-SeeMe Internet Videoconferencing Program
Internet Disaster Information Network
The Mercury Project Tele-Garden
Missouri Botanical Garden
Museum of Paleontology
NASA on the Internet
The Nine Planets Tour
Smithsonian Natural History Home Page
Whale Watching Web
Virtual Weather Maps & Satellite Images
Volcano World

Social Sciences/
Humanities

Classroom Connect on the Net
EdWeb
ERIC Educator Resources on the Web
Federal Bureau of Investigation (FBI)
Kids' Page
National Public Radio
White House Web
Wired

Vocational
Education

Career Mosaic
Directory of American Universities & Colleges
Edu.Net

INDEX

TIME, 143
Travel, 67, 146

United States
    American Civil War, 91
    Census Bureau, 71, 135
    cities, 63, 64
    Congress, 145
    FedWorld, 138
    geography, 63, 71
    maps, 65, 69, 71
    resources, 40, 46, 138
    State Department advisories, 146
    statistics, 63, 71, 135
    taxes, 27
    Virgin Islands, 63

Vatican City, 16
Vikings, 102
Vocational
    college bound, 150, 153
    entry level job seeker, 152
    financial aid, 155
    online career center, 153
    Peterson's Education Center, 155

Wall Street, 31
World Bank, 32
World Communities, 64, 66, 67
World Maps, 64, 66

Y

Yeats, William Butler, 43

Z

zines, 39

How to use the Internet in the K-12 classroom

The Internet Revealed
video series

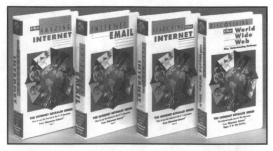

This landmark videotape production quickly delivers an A-to-Z understanding of what the Internet is and how to tap its unlimited educational resources. It's the one place students and teachers can turn for a thorough orientation and how-to-do-it instructions that get the beginner online. Tim McLain, nationally known writer/surfer for *Classroom Connect,* is your host for this easy-to-understand series of four top-of-the-line, movie-quality video productions. Tapes may be viewed as a set or individually in any order.

Tape 1: *The Amazing Internet* gives teachers and students a taste of the tremendous global teaching and learning power of the Internet. It introduces all of the communication, research, and navigation tools and the phenomenal World Wide Web. Captures and holds interest from start to finish! *Running time 25 minutes.*

Tape 2: *Internet Email* is the most versatile and commonly used communications tool. Here are clear step-by-step directions for using the power of electronic mail to join over 4,000 global discussion lists, collaborate on international projects, and communicate with teachers and students worldwide. *Running time 30 minutes.*

Tape 3: *Searching the Internet* teaches hands-on navigation skills and valuable searching techniques. Quickly and easily, learn to unlock the treasure trove of educational resources on the Internet. Includes gopher, Archie, Veronica, Jughead, principles of Boolean searching, and much more. Bonus section on WebCrawler, Lycos, Yahoo, and other World Wide Web search engines. *Running time 43 minutes.*

Tape 4: *Discovering the World Wide Web* opens the door to an incredible wealth of educational information. It's an up-to-the-minute teaching and learning tool of unparalleled scope. Easy-to-follow, step-by-step instructions show you how to navigate the Web and turn you into a World Wide Web power user. Includes a 20-minute tutorial on using NetScape. *Running time 58 minutes.*

Four VHS Videotapes
Complete set price: $150
Individual tapes: $39 each.

CLASSROOM CONNECT

1866 Colonial Village Lane
Lancaster, PA 17601
Phone: **(800) 638-1639**
Fax: **(717) 393-5752**
Email: **connect@wentworth.com**

The money's there for the technology you
need—you just have to know
who and how to ask!

Educator's Internet Funding Guide

$ $ $ $ $

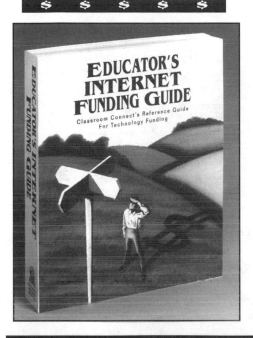

Here's how to find the funds you need to bring the Internet and other technology to your school. You'll learn how to successfully apply to government, corporate, and foundation sources, and discover powerful new techniques for developing an effective grassroots fund-raising campaign. This easy-to-understand guide is packed with the "do's and don'ts" of grant preparation, guidelines for assessing your funding needs, and tips for convincing potential funding sources of the importance of the Internet in your public or private school.

Two sections are worth the price of the entire guide:

- •A directory of hundreds of funding sources for your technology project includes: contact information, size of grants given, types of funding, subjects funded—and more.

- • A comprehensive 5-way cross index enables you to pinpoint the funding sources which are most likely to be responsive to your proposal.

Seasoned and novice grant writers are sure to appreciate this well-written, comprehensive desktop reference guide.

$44.95
1995, Softcover, Over 200 pages, Illustrated
ISBN 0-932577-13-X

1866 Colonial Village Lane, Lancaster, PA 17601
Phone: **(800) 638-1639** Fax: **(717) 393-5752**
Email: **connect@wentworth.com**

A clear road map to the educational resources on the Internet!

Educator's Internet Companion™

Whether you're a first-time Internet user or an experienced veteran, this book/diskette/videotape kit is jam-packed with information you need to tap into the Internet's almost unlimited educational resources.

This comprehensive guide clearly and concisely provides direct access to Internet material that brings study topics to life, makes learning fun, fosters independent research, and above all—educates!

You'll discover how to find thousands of lesson plans, documents, answers to questions—all with just a few keystrokes! You'll also find easy-to-understand directions for navigating the Internet without roadblocks or unexpected detours.

The **Educator's Internet Companion** includes:

Detailed reproducible lesson plans categorized by subject to help you integrate the Internet into the classroom.

An in-depth virtual tour of eight of the most fascinating and educationally rich sites on the Internet.

A World Wide Web tour that describes 50 of the top education-related Web sites.

Lists of hundreds of educational newsgroups and mailing lists.

Pointers to a host of educational resources on the Internet—with clear-cut directions on where and how to find them!

Internet basics tutorial that gives you in-depth instructions on how to use email, gopher, telnet, ftp, Archie, Veronica, the World Wide Web, and more!

$39.95
1995, Softcover, 289 pages, Illustrated
Included FREE with the purchase of the book, *NASA K-12 Internet Project* diskette, and *Global Quest: Internet in the Classroom* videotape.
ISBN 0-932577-10-5

 1866 Colonial Village Lane
Lancaster, PA 17601
Phone: **(800) 638-1639**
Fax: **(717) 393-5752**
Email: **connect@wentworth.com**